Checklists for Due Diligence

Checklists for Due Diligence

PETER HOWSON

Routledge
Taylor & Francis Group

LONDON AND NEW YORK

First published 2008 by Gower Publishing

Published 2016 by Routledge
2 Park Square, Milton Park, Abingdon, Oxon OX14 4RN
711 Third Avenue, New York, NY 10017, USA

Routledge is an imprint of the Taylor & Francis Group, an informa business

British Library Cataloguing in Publication Data
Howson, Peter, 1957–
    Checklists for due diligence
    1. Consolidation and merger of corporations – Law and
    legislation – Great Britain
    I. Title
    346.4'106626

    ISBN 9780566088629 (pbk)

Library of Congress Cataloging-in-Publication Data
Howson, Peter, 1957–
    Checklists for due diligence / by Peter Howson.
        p. cm.
    ISBN 0-566-08862-2
    1. Business enterprises--Purchasing. 2. Disclosure of information. I. Title.

    HD1393.25.H695 2008
    658.1'62--dc22

                                                                    2008005871

Contents

Introduction

Due diligence involves getting the answers to lots of questions in a short time. The checklists in this book provide most of the questions that a buyer could ask. The skill with checklists is using them wisely.

There is little likely to annoy a target more than being given a long list of questions that are not relevant, or being asked for the same information three or four times.

As every transaction is different, not all of the questions will be appropriate for every deal. The checklists should be edited and modified for the transaction rather than used blindly. The areas to cover and the depth of coverage are a matter of judgement and depend on a buyer's knowledge and how much risk he or she attaches to areas where his or her knowledge is limited.

Also, the checklists in this book overlap. For example the financial due diligence checklist contains questions about employees and tax, but there are also separate checklists covering human resources and tax. It is up to the purchaser to use whichever are appropriate.

The best way of keeping the checklists relevant is to keep the objectives of due diligence in mind. Given the Anglo-Saxon principle of 'caveat emptor' and statistics which suggest that most acquisitions fail, due diligence is useful to the purchaser in four ways:

1. As an aid to identifying potential liabilities.

2. As a supplement to the legal protection that may be obtainable against those potential liabilities.

3. As an aid to ensuring a successful transaction.

4. To supply complete and reliable data in a public offering.

AS AN AID TO IDENTIFYING POTENTIAL LIABILITIES

As a general principle, negotiations between buyer and seller seek to apportion liabilities between the two parties. Liabilities whose origin is pre-transaction belong to the seller and those whose origin are post-transaction belong to the buyer. One of the basic aims of due diligence is to help the buyer identify those potential liabilities so that it can deal with them in negotiations.

AS A SUPPLEMENT TO THE LEGAL PROTECTION THAT MAY BE OBTAINABLE AGAINST THOSE POTENTIAL LIABILITIES

There are three problems with relying on contractual protection such as warranties:

1. Difficulties of proving either that there has been a breach or that there has been a loss resulting from it.

2. A warranty will not normally apply if breaches of the topic in question have been disclosed.

3. A guarantee is only as good as its giver. If the sellers are not particularly creditworthy or have moved their assets to an offshore jurisdiction, getting them to pay up may be difficult if not impossible.

Comparatively speaking, due diligence is cheap, litigation is not. This is why buyers are more comfortable knowing about problems beforehand rather than being left with the possibility, however remote, of making warranty or indemnity claims or having to sue the seller after completion.

AS AN AID TO ENSURING A SUCCESSFUL TRANSACTION

Most acquisitions fail to deliver the benefits expected of them. Due diligence should be structured not just to get the deal done but also to maximise the chances of a successful transaction. A common mistake is to be too obsessed with the financials to the detriment of other areas. Due diligence should be an aid to understanding the business being bought, its business model, the market in which it operates and, therefore, its prospects. Acquisitions where cost cutting is the only objective are rarely successful. An integration plan which shows how the benefits are to be delivered should be developed in advance. Due diligence can provide a lot of the data and analysis needed.

TO SUPPLY COMPLETE AND RELIABLE DATA IN A PUBLIC OFFERING

Due diligence for an offering of securities is different than for an acquisition. The focus is on complete and reliable information so that sponsors do not misrepresent to potential buyers.

A due diligence programme should have five strands which the checklists should reflect:

1.   The verification of assets and liabilities.

2.   The identification and quantification of risks.

3.   The protection needed against such risks which will in turn feed into the negotiations.

4.   The identification of upside potential and synergy benefits.

5.   A strong input into post-acquisition planning.

And due diligence should address the 'soft' issues such as cultural compatibility and management succession as well as the 'hard' issues such as the legals and financials.

Much of the information will come from interviews. Open ended questions are best. Ask the question. Shut up. Listen. Bad interviewers are the ones who spend forever asking the question then end up answering it themselves. Where interviews are face to face it is useful to have two interviewers; one to listen to the answers and one to watch the body language.

A popular misconception of due diligence is that it is a process of enquiry designed to unearth deal breakers. This should not be what due diligence is about. Any deal breakers should be addressed before detailed negotiations begin and the parties engage expensive advisers.

Finally, do not be fooled into thinking that a process driven checklist approach to due diligence is the answer. Most important of all is understanding. Buyers have to have a process and checklists are very useful, but the objective is not just to ask the right questions but to achieve a real understanding of the target company.

Buyer Pre-Due Diligence

The sensible starting point for due diligence is due diligence on yourself, the buyer. However stupid that may sound at first, simple answers to some of the more obvious questions can help prevent wasting a lot of time, money and effort.

What is the business strategy?

How do acquisitions fit into the business strategy?

Does the target fit the strategy?

Have we carried out sufficient pre-acquisition planning?

Are we sufficiently prepared for the due diligence exercise?

- Who is managing the process on our side?

- Which areas are we going to investigate? Why?

- Are we giving enough attention to the 'soft' areas like culture and management?

- Do we know what we really need to know in each area of investigation?

- Do we have enough time to complete the process? If not, what are we going to do about it?

Do we have the information to brief advisers properly?

Where are the synergies going to come from? Have we tried to quantify them in detail? What further information is needed?

Have we set a walk away price?

Have we worked out an adequate implementation plan especially for the human resources issues? For example:

- How will individuals be chosen to fill available positions?
    - What are the selection criteria?
    - Who will make the decision?
- Will incentives be needed to keep talent in place?
- When will we work out who will be surplus to requirements?
- Have we worked out the termination packages and the timing of terminations?
- Have we a communication plan in place to deal with staff changes?

Have we considered any organizational re-design opportunities the acquisition creates, for example outsourcing as an alternative to in-house resources?

Have we explored all the consequences of the deal, for example the effects on current operations, existing personnel, the industry and competitors?

What is our attitude to risk? Is this the same for all types of risk?

Have we set materiality limits for the due diligence investigation?

Have we explained the process to the seller?

Have we agreed access to people and documents with the seller?

Are we clear on what we want from whom, when and in what form?

2 Selecting (and Working with) Advisers

Discuss the proposed acquisition internally and due diligence with those most likely to be involved in and affected by it.

Make sure everyone who needs to understand is clear about what due diligence is about and the advantages of bringing in advisers and what they are expected to do.

DECIDE

- On a timetable.
- Who will manage the process.
- Who will be the main contact for the advisers.
- Whether to set up a management team/steering group.
- Who will prepare and agree the initial briefs.
- Who will choose the advisers and on what criteria.
- How to keep everyone in touch with the progress of the acquisition/ due diligence process.
- What the main concerns are.
- What due diligence needs to be carried out.
- The key issues and main areas of concern for each area of due diligence.
- Whether due diligence ought to be phased, for example by carrying out commercial due diligence before commissioning the more expensive financial and legal due diligence.

Identify the problems that may arise during the course of the due diligence process and during the course of working with your advisers.

Ask potential advisers to sign confidentiality agreements then discuss the proposed transaction with them drawing on any previous experience they may have of this type of transaction. Get an idea of costs and timescales.

Draw up a high level scope for due diligence which covers the issues you feel need to be covered and send to potential advisers with a request for formal proposals.

Compile a criteria checklist for choosing advisers.

Check references, if given.

Check that advisers have understood the brief.

DISCUSS FURTHER WITH THE MOST PROMISING ADVISERS ONCE PROPOSALS ARE RECEIVED

- Who will do the work and how many will be involved?

- What is their relevant experience? Relevant experience of the individuals counts for far more than the relevant experience of the organization.

- What is the methodology for the job?

- What is the fee and its structure, for example fixed price vs time based. Is/should a proportion should be contingent?

- Should payments be linked to completion of specific stages in the work?

- Make sure you meet the person/persons who will carry out the due diligence and those that will be your principal contacts.

AFTER DISCUSSIONS

- Eliminate those not suitable.

- Compare strengths and weaknesses, include composition of the team and previous relevant due diligence experience.

- Compare proposed fees and estimated timescales.

- Check any points that are unclear.

- Assess genuine interest, commitment and professionalism of those interviewed.

- Decide which you like and with whom you get on well.

AGREE THE FINAL BRIEF

- Discuss your initial brief and the adviser's proposal and refine final brief.

- Agree on the timescale, how fees and costs will be calculated and paid.

ON APPOINTMENT

- Draw up written terms of reference for each adviser and use these as the basis for a contract for both parties to sign.

- Inform all those that need to know when work will commence and who is to be the main contact for the advisers.

- Make arrangements (allocate a person) to provide the advisers with information, equipment and the space they require.

- Make sure advisers know who else is advising and what they are doing.

MANAGE THE ADVISERS THROUGHOUT THE PROCESS

- Keep in close contact with your advisers.

- Have regular feedback sessions.

- Make sure arrangements for working with your advisers are running smoothly.

RECEIVING THE RESULTS

- Decide how you want the advisers to report their recommendations and conclusions to you.

- Check the report's accuracy and conclusions before making it available to others within your organization.

ASSESS THE OUTCOME

- Consider if you have got what you asked for, in the form you wanted it and its value to your decision making.

- Discuss the report with your advisers and its implications, and negotiate amendments or additions where the report fails to meet the agreed brief.

AFTER DUE DILIGENCE

- Decide if you want further advice or guidance and on what financial basis that might be given.

- Approve and implement any specific recommendations.

3 Briefing Advisers

Circulate code words for transaction and the parties involved. 11

Give the names/details of companies/assets being acquired.

What is the type of transaction, in other words assets deal, share deal or a mixture?

Which companies are to be investigated?

What period should be reviewed? It might be different for different areas.

Give a description/history of the target company.

Provide copies of the target's:

- Product and company literature.

- Group structure.

- Sale memorandum (if there is one).

- Business plan (if there is one).

Communicate the timetable.

Circulate copies of confidentiality agreements.

Outline which advisers are doing what.

Publish an 'all parties' contact list.

Set out the reasons for the acquisition:

- Strategic rationale.

- Other perceived benefits.

Is the transaction driven by technology considerations? If using outside experts to evaluate technology, how will the know-how they investigate be protected?

Circulate copies of any internal papers justifying the deal.

Specify materiality limits.

Communicate post-acquisition plans:

- Planned asset sales.

- Planned business closures.

- Development plans (when, where and timescales/priorities).

- To what extent will the target be integrated? Over what timescale?

Summarize your existing knowledge.

Summarize your concerns (both pre- and post-acquisition).

Communicate for whom due diligence reports are to be written (Board, bankers etc.).

Communicate what report format is required.

Draw up written terms of reference for each adviser (if not already provided):

- Financial due diligence. Who is covering IT, tax and pensions?

- Legal due diligence. Who is covering antitrust, environmental, human resources, property and intellectual property?

- Commercial due diligence. Who is covering operational, technical and management?

4

Information to be Requested from the Target

INFORMATION REQUEST LIST

Information	Due diligence topic
Accounting Policies Copies of last two years auditors' management letters. Copies of accounting manuals. Are all key accounting policies disclosed in the Annual Financial Statements? Have they changed recently? Have reported profits been affected by changes in accounting policies?	**Financial**
Accounts Copies of audited accounts for the last three years. Copy of the latest management accounts. List of year-end journals and reconciliation between management and statutory accounts.	**Financial**
Agreements	
Copies of: • Agreements with major customers. • Distribution contracts, including all agreements with independent sales representatives, distributors and franchisees. • Warranty agreements. • Contracts with suppliers. • Subcontractor agreements. • Partnership or joint venture agreements of any partnership in which target or any subsidiary is a member. • Sponsorship agreements.	**Legal**

• Property lease and maintenance agreements entered into by the target. • All leases and tenancies granted by the target along with details of tenants and terms and assignment of leases where the target or a subsidiary company was the original lessee.	**Legal, property**
• Standard service agreements, employee terms and conditions, union agreements, management contracts, termination contracts, golden parachute and profit share agreements, employment agency contracts and consulting agreements.	**Legal, human resources, management**
• All contracts relating to the acquisition or disposal of companies or businesses during the last six years.	**Legal, tax**
• Hire purchase, lease and rental agreements. • Loan agreements.	**Legal, financial**
• All agreements dealing with intellectual property rights, including licensing agreements (in both directions, i.e. both by and to the target).	**Intellectual property, legal**
Antitrust Information required to file with appropriate antitrust authorities. All covenants not to compete, confidentiality agreements and other restrictive agreements. Details of membership of, and representation on, any trade associations or other industry bodies such as standards committees.	**Antitrust**
Capital commitments	
Details of the current capital expenditure budget. Has there been significant CAPEX over the past three years? Are any major CAPEX requirements expected in the next three years? Details of any capital commitments.	**Financial**
Details of any contingent liabilities.	**Financial, legal**
Cash flow A summary of the month-end bank and cash book position for the current year and previous two years. Copies of the latest bank reconciliation with supporting bank statement. An explanation of the major variations in the net cash position over the last three years. An explanation of intra-month variation in the net cash position. Is the overall pattern of cash flow affected by seasonal factors? Are there any exceptional cash inflows or outflows? What are the principal uses of cash generated by operations?	**Financial**

Compliance Does the business comply with generally accepted standards of corporate governance (such as Cadbury, Greenbury and Turnbull)? Has the target complied with statutory requirements to file documents at Companies House? In particular, have all charges on the company's assets been properly recorded and filed?	**Legal, financial**
Consents Details of all licences or consents, permits or authorities necessary to carry on business. Copies of reports or other documents filed with governmental agencies that have regulatory power over the target or a subsidiary.	**Legal, financial, environmental**
Contingent liabilities Are there any contingent liabilities (e.g. guarantees, warranties)? Are there material future commitments under rental/operating lease agreements?	**Financial**

Corporate records and structure
Exact corporate name.
Address.
Memorandum and Articles of Association, and all amendments of target and each subsidiary of target.
Location of certificate of incorporation.
Location of all statutory books of the target and its subsidiaries.
Is the target UK resident?
Is the target a close company? If so, has it made any loans to participants?
Legal structure of company and subsidiaries:
• A list, with details, of all dormant, joint venture, subsidiary, group and associate companies.
• A family tree showing the relationship between them and ownership chain to ultimate beneficial owners.
• Details of any branch, place of business or substantial assets outside the UK.
• Details during the last [six] years of any:
   – incorporations;
   – acquisitions;
   – disposals;
   – joint ventures or strategic alliances;
   – windings up.
Minutes of all Board of Directors', committee and shareholders' meetings.
Material information or documents furnished to shareholders and to directors during the last two years.
	Legal, tax, financial

Customers Degree of customer concentration. Evidence of customer satisfaction. Significant customers lost/won in last three years? Are special terms given to any customers? Management's assessment of customers' key purchase criteria (KPC).	**Commercial, financial**
Debt Details of all borrowing facilities (amount, repayment or conversion terms, interest rates, covenants and copies of trust deeds) including loan agreements, notes, mortgages and security agreements and all financing arrangements, including sale and leaseback arrangements, capital leases and hire purchases including security or guarantees given. Details of charges over assets of the group. Copies of correspondence with lenders. Details of any debt arrangements, guarantees or indemnification between officers, directors or the shareholder(s) and the company. Are there any loans from shareholders or connected parties that could be repayable in the short term? Schedule of loans made giving details of borrower, authority for loan, amount due, security, interest and repayment terms. Details of any financial guarantee or indemnities given to secure credit to third parties. Has the target applied for or received any government grants? Are borrowing facilities appropriate to cash requirements?	**Legal, financial**
Dispensations Has a resolution been passed by the target or any group company to take advantage of any of the dispensations contained in the 1985 Companies Act, i.e. to dispense with: • Accounts before an AGM. • Annual appointment of auditors. • Holding AGMs. • The need to renew the duration of an authority to allot shares and debentures beyond five years.	**Legal**
Disputes Details of any disputes, e.g. with: • customers; • suppliers; • subcontractors; • employees; • neighbours.	**Legal, financial**
Distribution A list of licensing or distribution agreements. Names of any selling agents and a summary of goods sold by them.	**Legal, intellectual property, commercial, financial, antitrust**

Employee information – directors & senior managers	
Profile of each director and senior manager: • Previous experience before joining business. • Qualifications and degrees. • Duties throughout the period under review. • Age. • Years of service and date of appointment to Board (if applicable). • Current remuneration. • Service agreements. • Pension arrangements. • Other benefits (e.g. use of company car), share options/ incentive arrangements. • Directorships of companies that carry on business of any kind with the target or its subsidiaries. • Details of any restrictive covenants, confidentiality provisions and 'golden parachutes'.	**Management, legal, human resources, financial, pension, taxation**
Copy of documented organization chart. If none, why not? Does the management team meet regularly to review business performance? Are these meetings minuted? Details of management succession plans.	**Management, human resources**
Are any payments made to senior managers' wives, related parties or related companies?	**Tax**
List of former directors and senior executives who have left during the last three years, with brief details.	**Commercial**
Employee information – staff	
Details of all staff including date of birth, age, date of commencement of employment, length of service, salary, benefits, notice period, department and location. Copy of any union agreements and list of staff in each trade union. Details of employee representatives, who they are and who they represent, terms of office, etc. What is the industrial relations record of the business? Details of: • Dismissals, including redundancies in the last six months. • Disciplinary and grievance procedures and all recent instances of their use. • Sickness records. Details of arrangements to be followed in the event of redundancies. List of part-time and disabled employees. Details of employees on sick leave, maternity leave or secondment. Details of employees employed on fixed-term, temporary and casual contracts. Details of staff turnover rates. Are they low or high by industry standards? What is the trend?	**Human resources**

Brief outline of salary/wage payment structure, management levels and staff grading system. Copies of personnel policies. Copies of staff manuals and employee handbooks. Holiday pay arrangements. Any promised changes to terms and conditions, including pending pay increases. Details of employees' average weekly hours. List of employees who have opted out of the Working Time Regulations. Details of training spend. Are the growth prospects of the business threatened by skill shortages?	**Human resources, financial, intellectual property**
Details of any consultants or other people such as agents who provide regular services.	**Human resources, intellectual property**
Details of any correspondence with: • Commission for Racial Equality. • The Data Protection Commissioner. • Disability Commission. • Equal Opportunities Commission. • Any Health and Safety Authority.	**Human resources**
Environmental Details of past environmental assessments. Copies of any notices of environmental claims, violations, prosecutions, employee claims/complaints or insurance claims. Copies of correspondence with environmental regulators or third parties.	**Environmental**
History Brief account of history, location and nature of business.	**All**
Information systems	
Copies of consultancy reports on internal systems and controls. Are the management information systems fully integrated? Is the business dependent on third parties for software/hardware maintenance? Have systems' weaknesses been noted in auditors' management letters? Are the management information systems producing timely and reliable information?	**Financial, IT**
What key performance indicators does the business use to monitor its performance? Are there systems to ensure effective cash management?	**Financial**
Confirmation that the company's systems, software and technology is owned solely by the company and does not infringe on any other party's rights.	**Legal, IT**

Insolvency Has any order been made, or resolution passed, for the winding up of the target or any subsidiary? Has any administration order been made, or any petition for such an order presented in respect of the target or any group company?	**Legal**
Insurance Schedule or copies of all material insurance policies covering property, liabilities and operations, including product liabilities. Schedule of any other insurance policies in force such as 'key man' policies or director indemnification policies. All other relevant documents pertaining to the company's insurance and liability exposure. Have the levels of insurance cover been reviewed recently?	**Risk management, financial, legal, environmental**
Inter-group transactions	
Schedule listing all inter-company balances, both debit and credit. Classify between trading, management charges, rent, interest, etc. and financing.	**Financial, taxation**
Details of intra-group assets transfers. Details of group tax matters, e.g. group income election, VAT grouping. Copy of transfer pricing policy. Management assessment of practice. Have there been any intra-group transactions not at an arm's length basis?	**Taxation**
Intellectual property Details of all patents, trademarks and copyrights granted or applied for showing countries covered and, for applications outstanding, an estimate of likely date of grant. Details of inventors/authors. Details of other IPRs, e.g. domain names or unregistered IPRs such as copyright. Does management believe it has all necessary patents, trademarks and IPR? Are there any restrictions or limitations on the use of IPRs or third party ownership rights? Details of: • Any trade secrets. • Licences and other agreements to which the target is a party. Revenue streams or royalty obligations associated with each licence. • Any non-disclosure agreements. • Any challenges to intellectual property rights, any infringement claims and all litigation involving IPRs. • Procedures for ensuring that IPRs are protected. • Current R&D projects. Management's assessment of the likelihood of such projects giving rise to a patentable invention. • Maintenance fees for patents and trademarks. • Employment agreements relating to IPRs.	**Intellectual property, legal, human resources**

Litigation	
Details of any litigation, actual, threatened or pending. A summary of any administrative proceedings, governmental investigations, or inquiries against or involving the target or any subsidiary. Copies of correspondence with customers or suppliers relating to complaints or disputes. Details of any disputes with suppliers, competitors or customers. How frequently has the business been involved in litigation in the past?	**Legal**
Are there any outstanding employment claims such as discrimination and wrongful dismissal cases? Please do not limit to employment tribunal proceedings.	**Human resources, legal**
Marketing What is the marketing strategy? Has advertising/sales promotion spend or direction changed recently?	**Commercial, financial**
Markets and competitors Information on market and competitors, including market shares, competitor profiles, who are the winners and losers, why? Do any have a lead technologically or otherwise? Management's assessment of markets. Size? Are markets expanding? Are there new products/geographical markets to attack? How price sensitive are customers? Is this true of all of them? What are the major factors driving the size and growth of the markets? Barriers to entry? What R&D/development would be needed to improve the target's competitive position or take it into new markets? Legislation/regulation. Competitive forces – e.g. consolidation, restructuring, diversification. How cyclical is the market? Impact of economic variables, e.g. recession, interest rates, exchange rates. Market positioning vs. competitors. Sources of competitive advantage.	**Commercial, financial**
Operations/production Brief description of the production methods and techniques and the relative position of the business in relation to the 'leading edge' in the industry in which it operates. Summary of recent production problems. Constraints on production capacity. Immediate CAPEX requirements.	**Commercial, financial**
Pension Summary of pension arrangements. Details of pension or retirement schemes, including a copy of the trust deed and rules (including amendments), members' explanatory booklets and any announcements, the latest scheme accounts and accounts for the previous year, list of members, latest and previous actuarial reports, copies of any correspondence on latest actuarial position.	**Pensions, financial**

Please confirm that CA approval has been obtained and that there is no OPRA interest. Are defined benefit schemes fully funded? Are equal pay and increases provided for? Details of any unfounded pension commitments.	
Product information	
Product catalogues and price lists.	**All**
Copies of any recent industry or product surveys. Copies of any recent reports on the target or its products produced by the target or a third party. Management's description of products' role in the value chain, any complementary products and services and alternative applications for products and services. Management's assessment of strengths and weaknesses of key products and services.	**Commercial, financial, technical**
Description of the product improvement process. How often is each product updated? What triggers a new product release? Access to product complaint letters and recent lost sales reports.	**Commercial, technical**
Details of product/service warranties and provisions for such warranties.	**Financial, legal**
Does the product incorporate any third party intellectual property such as shareware?	**Legal, intellectual property, technical**
Projections and forecasts	
Are regular budgets produced, are variances monitored and are budgets updated during the year? A copy of the current year's budget and estimate of trading results for the current year. Copies of profit and loss and cash flow projections (one–two years) together with underlying assumptions. Have budgets/forecasts in the last two years been accurate? If not, what reasons do management give for this? Have the projections been prepared especially for the due diligence review or are they normal operating budgets? Were operational as well as financial staff involved in their preparation? Do the projections assume any changes in accounting policies or bases? Are reductions being projected in stock levels or debtor days? Justification? Are increases being projected in creditor days? Justification? Have the projections been approved by the Board? Are there any projected cost savings that depend upon future actions?	**Financial**

Details of any medium term (three–five year) forecasts. Are projected sales levels higher than recent/current levels? Is projected sales growth consistent with industry growth? To what extent are they reliant on something new, such as: • market share gains; • new products; • new markets/new market segments; • new major customers; • new sources of supply. Is projected sales growth volume- or price-based? How sensitive is the target's performance to external factors such as: • economic cycle; • fashion; • proposed legislation. Are projected changes in gross margins supported by known price rises, cost reductions or firmly priced orders/contracts?	**Financial, commercial**
Property	
Details of premises used by the target giving complete address, a description of its function, terms of ownership, location, size, description, dilapidation clauses, rent and rates payable and any recent valuations carried out. Do recent valuations differ significantly from book value? Sight of any recent independent or internal valuations or insurance reports. Copies of all appraisals.	**Legal, property**
Copies of any dilapidation schedules served and presented by landlords. Details of past payments of rent and rates with a summary of amounts outstanding or prepaid. Comments on availability of any spare land. Details of any premises not currently in use. Management's assessment of future premises requirements.	**Legal, property, financial**
Are the directors aware of any environmental problems? Copies of all studies, site evaluations, and governmental filings and reports prepared by consultants or employees concerning the presence of hazardous materials or toxic substances on, under or about any property owned or leased by target or any subsidiary.	**Legal, property, financial, environmental**
Purchasing and supply	
Degree of supplier concentration. Details of alternative arrangements for important materials which are currently single sourced. Have disruptions in supply arisen recently? Details of subcontractors. Are subcontracting arrangements well established, with alternative suppliers in place? Have there been any recent changes in subcontractors?	**Operational, financial**

What factors affect the price of purchases and are prices generally stable? Are there alternative sources of supply? Are there any unusual payment terms to suppliers? Are there any contracted forward purchase commitments? Are volume rebate agreements in place?	**Financial**
Are any purchases made on a non-arm's length basis?	**Financial, taxation**
Please supply details of technology, etc. licensed by the company.	**Legal, intellectual property, commercial, financial**
Regulatory Is the business subject to any regulatory matters, e.g. government quotas or consents, health and safety, consumer credit, licensing or price controls?	**Legal, operational, environmental, human resources**
Research and development (R&D)	
Is the research and development function integrated with production? If so, how?	**Financial, IT, technical**
Has the R&D function been successful in the past?	**Financial, intellectual property, commercial**
Sales	
List of major customers with whom there are agreements and summary of those agreements. Are there agency agreements?	**Legal, financial, commercial, antitrust**
Details of membership of any trade association or professional body and of any code of practice or any other rights or obligations imposed by such membership.	**Legal, antitrust, financial, commercial**
Has the sales mix changed over the last three years? If so, why? Have returns, guarantee or warranty claims increased recently?	**Financial, commercial**
Are there any exceptional/non-recurring revenues? Have unit prices increased or come under severe pressure? Degree to which discounting is a regular trading feature. Has the basis of calculating discounts changed in the last three years? Are sales seasonal? Impact of exchange rate movements on pricing?	**Financial**
Extent of sales to related parties.	**Financial, taxation**
Are any sales made on a non-arm's length basis?	**Taxation**
How is the sales force motivated/rewarded?	**Financial, commercial, human resources**

Shares and shareholders Authorised and issued shares of target and each subsidiary. Description of shares. Rights of each class of share capital. Details of any shares created or issued in the last [six] years. Details of any other changes in share capital in the last [six] years. Details of any issue of, or proposals to issue, share capital since the last year-end. Are there any unusual reserves or restrictions on distributions to shareholders? Have any distributions been made or promised since the last accounts? Has the company ever redeemed any shares or debentures from profits or reserves? Is any interest treated as a distribution for tax purposes? Names of shareholders and holdings. Are any shareholders under any legal disability (e.g. as a result of mental illness)? Do any of the major shareholders have any interests in other businesses which could be in competition with the target? Are there warrants, options and other rights to acquire shares? Details of stock options, stock purchase and other employee benefit plans and agreements. Copies of shareholder agreements. Are there any encumbrances over shares? Copies of all correspondence and other communications with shareholders.	**Legal, taxation, financial**
Strategy Copy of any business plans in existence. What is the essence of the company strategy? Who is involved in setting the strategy? When was the strategy last updated? Has the strategy changed recently? Have external consultants advised on strategy?	**Commercial, financial**
Tangible fixed assets General description, including age categorised by type of plant and machinery (or copy of fixed asset register). Are there any recent independent asset valuation reports? Have any new capital commitments been taken on since the last accounts?	**Financial**
Has any interest, own labour or materials been capitalised? Details of all investments in other companies.	**Financial, taxation**
List of all motor vehicles owned, leased or hired and users' names.	**Financial, management human resources**
Taxation Summarise tax provisions for the last [three]/[six] years. Reconcile the tax charge shown in the accounts to the prevailing statutory rates. Describe deferred tax provisioning policy.	**Taxation**

Are recent tax computations agreed by the Inland Revenue? If not, what issues are outstanding or being disputed by the Inland Revenue? Are there any years still open?

Has the company been engaged in any schemes for tax avoidance? If so, please give details and copies of any related documentation (e.g. legal opinion).

What is the status of overseas tax audits? What have been the previous outcomes of such tax audits?

Describe relations with the tax authorities. Have submissions always been on time? Has tax always been paid on time? Has the company ever been subject to penalties? Has the company ever been investigated by the tax authorities?

Details of any correspondence with the Inland Revenue/local tax authorities.

Copy of the tax computation and correspondence, covering the last three/six years.

Are any concessionary tax treatments being followed?

Copy of any apportionment clearances which have been obtained.

Is there a backlog of tax payable to any authority?

Has the business entered into any tax planning schemes in recent years?

Are any agreed tax losses restricted in their availability?

Summarise any past rollover/holdover claims that impact on tax base cost of significant assets.

Copies of Industrial Buildings Allowance history.

Confirm all relevant elections have been validly made on time.

Copies of all tax clearances sought/received.

Confirm VAT status.

Copy of VAT returns for the current year and previous year.

A copy of the VAT account (including VAT bad debt account), PAYE and NIC account.

If member of a group, confirm that VAT and corporation tax implications of management charges, etc. have been considered.

Document any special arrangements and compliance with them.

Confirm VAT payments and returns are up to date with no default surcharge notices.

Details of the latest control visits by PAYE, DSS and VAT authorities and the outcome.

Copies of the latest P11Ds. Copies of any P11D dispensations.

Details of any taxation or stamp duty schemes.

Has the company been party to any transactions where Section 765 Income and Corporation Taxes Act 1988 could apply? (This requires UK companies to obtain consent from the Treasury before certain transactions can be carried out by overseas subsidiaries.)

Has the company made any claims under double tax relief treaties?

Does the company have unremittable overseas income or gains?

Have all relevant documents been duly stamped? Does the company have any exposure to Stamp Duty Reserve Tax?

Trading results – historic	
Details of the latest order book (with comparative figures). Monthly totals of sales for the current year and previous two years. Monthly gross profit percentage for current year and previous two years. Have gross profit percentages changed? If so, why? Analysis of purchases from principal suppliers for last three years. Basis of allocation of costs between different subsidiaries, activities, or divisions?	**Financial**
Analysis of turnover by main product groups for last three years. Analysis of turnover by main customers and geographical markets for last three years.	**Financial, commercial**
Analysis of intra-group trading for the past [three] years and whether on normal commercial terms.	**Financial, tax**
Trading results – current Since the last accounts date, details of any of: • Significant changes in the nature or scale of the business compared with the previous year. • Any transactions or liabilities entered into other than in the normal course of trading. • Any material adverse change in turnover or financial or trading position. • Anything done by the target to prejudice its own goodwill. • Any abnormal factors affecting the business. • Details of all foreign exchange contracts open at, and opened since, the last accounts date to which the target is a party. • Details of all letters of credit in issue at, or issued since, the last accounts. What is the impact on recent profitability of provisions being created or released?	**Financial**
Working capital – cash Is the level of cash at the balance sheet date representative of the cash held throughout the month/year? What are the overdraft facilities? How is surplus cash managed?	**Financial**
What are the terms of bank loans/overdrafts?	**Financial, legal**
Working capital – stocks Particulars of basis of valuation of stocks and work in progress at each year-end. Have stock qualities been physically verified recently? What levels of stock loss have arisen on recent stock counts? How are obsolete and slow moving stock provisions calculated at the year end and at intermediate dates? Have stock levels increased or decreased? Why?	**Financial**

Working capital – debtors	**Financial**
Most recent aged listing of trade debtors. Is the ageing of trade debtors improving or deteriorating, and is it acceptable?	
Is the business vulnerable to one or two large debtors defaulting?	
Summary of current bad debt provisions. What is the past experience of bad debts?	
Are normal credit terms being enforced with all customers?	
Are there any unusual sundry debtors or prepayments?	
Schedule of accruals showing the basis upon which these have been calculated.	
Working capital – trade creditors	**Financial**
Most recent aged list of trade creditors.	
Are there any unusual sundry creditors or accruals?	
Is the business under pressure to pay creditors more quickly?	
Do any creditor balances attract interest or offer discounts for early payment?	
How is deferred income calculated?	

Financial Due Diligence

OBJECTIVES

The fundamental building blocks of financial due diligence (FDD) are:

- Giving confidence in the underlying performance.

- Verifying the numbers on which the offer is based.

- Providing ammunition for the negotiations/identifying where warranties/indemnities are needed.

Giving confidence in the underlying performance

Financial due diligence (FDD) aims to provide an assessment of 'maintainable profit'. Maintainable profit is the underlying profit which the target company is capable of earning. Accounting is not a science. This means that all accounts are subject to a number of judgements. Some can make a big difference to reported profitability. Calculating maintainable profit means undoing what has been done by other accountants. It also means removing any 'one-off' profits or expenses which distort the profitability of the business. Only a small part of arriving at underlying profit derives from standardizing accounting policies and removing any one-offs. It is much more about assessing the means by which profits are generated, which in turn means understanding the market, customers, production, suppliers and management, and identifying factors key to the success of the business.

Of course, it is quite possible that the numbers have been cobbled together or achieved more by luck than skill. For these reasons it is also an important function of FDD to review the reliability of the systems recording those profits.

Verifying the numbers on which the offer is based

Financial due diligence is not the same as an audit. FDD reports what the numbers are and why they are what they are, whereas an audit confirms that the numbers are correct. In other words, the aim of an audit is to verify results. Due diligence seeks to explain results.

Until a firm offer is made for the business, the seller will have controlled information. Anything provided will have presented the target company in its best light. The would-be purchaser will have based its offer on a multiple of last year's profit and will have made a number of assumptions such as:

- The future performance of the business will be similar to the past.
- The relationships with customers are strong and this will continue.
- Margins are not under pressure.
- Accounting policies have been consistent and reasonably applied.
- There are no looming liabilities such as significantly higher maintenance costs.

Financial due diligence gives the acquirer the opportunity to satisfy itself that the assumptions it has used in its assessment and valuation of the business are reasonable. It also provides a view on underlying profitability which will form the basis for forecasting future performance.

Identifying items for which warranties/indemnities may be needed

Deal breakers should have been dealt with long before expensive advisers are engaged. Inevitably, though, there will be a number of liabilities or uncertainties that could be liabilities, for which a buyer will seek legal protection. These may include:

- Over/under valuation of assets and liabilities.
- Adequacy of provisions.
- Potential black holes, for example pensions.

5

Financial Due Diligence

EXECUTIVE SUMMARY

Provide a short executive summary dealing with the main financial risks and opportunities for the buyer in doing this deal, along with an assessment of the likelihood of those risks materializing and the costs if they do. Summarize what warranty/indemnity protection should be negotiated, along with and indication of the priority for each point.

HISTORY AND COMMERCIAL ACTIVITIES

Provide a short history and development of the target and the activities undertaken along with a description of the group's activities and its commercial objectives and policies:

- Origins of the business.

- Principal events in the last ten years such as changes in ownership, products and services, management and competition.

Outline the target's corporate structure:

- Share capital and ownership.

- Nature of share capital, details of shareholders, rights attaching to different classes of shares, together with options and warrants.

- Legal structure.

- Explanation of group structure, details of share capital for main subsidiaries and any minority interest.

- Management structure.

Much of the factual information here overlaps with legal. The value the accountants can add from their management interviews is to paint a picture of how the target really works. Changes in management and shareholdings can happen for perfectly understandable reasons. They can also happen for reasons which an acquirer would find interesting. An acquirer does not need financial due diligence to report on this type of thing but as reporting accountants spend a good deal of time on site and speak to most of the management, they make good observers of what really goes on.

Give a breakdown of turnover by categories for the last [three] years and, where possible, an assessment of the size and development of the principal markets in which the target operates, its main customer type, potential customers and assessment of market share:

- Sales and gross profit by activity and geography.

- Overall trends in sales or gross margins with brief explanation (the detailed analysis will be given in the Trading Performance review below).

- Trends in market sizes, shares and growth.

- Description of major competitors.

- Target's positioning vis-à-vis the competition.

- The sustainability of sales and margin in each area of activity and in each geographical market.

- Proposed new products and markets.

- Barriers to entry.

- Threats and opportunities.

Summarize any new activities planned, recently commenced or terminated.

Provide details of trade associations, bonding arrangements, etc.

SALES AND MARKETING

The aim is to report on any vulnerabilities. A heavy dependence on a few customers is an obvious cause for concern, as are long-term agency agreements if the acquirer is planning to integrate the business. Customer dissatisfaction is another area to probe. Credit notes, unpaid bills, invoice disputes and warranty claims can all be evidence of something fundamentally wrong with the business and its ability to maintain market share. Related interviews, say with the sales force, will confirm the state of customer relationships. Discounting or an exceptional level of advertising/promotion may well have massaged recent business performance. Areas for investigation include:

- Customer base – profile by geographic region, industry type and any other appropriate criteria.

- Analysis of sales and gross profit by major customers/customer groups over the previous three–five years.

- Extent of customer dependencies/major contracts.

- Stability, reliability and sustainability of business with major customers/customer groups.

- Strategies for:
  - marketing;
  - pricing – leader or follower, how often prices reviewed, ability to flex;
  - sales;
  - advertising;
  - distribution

- Organization of the sales and marketing functions.

- Details of selling methods including incentive schemes and the use of agents.

- Standard terms (discounts, credit terms, warranty).

- Seasonality of sales.

- Effectiveness of the sales and marketing function.

PURCHASING AND SUPPLIES

Outline the target's relationships with suppliers, assess the relative importance of each major source of supply and provide details of any particular commercial relationships.

Underlying profit could be severely affected in a business where there are unstable prices, a dependency on a few suppliers, frequent disruptions and no alternative supply sources. The picture could be worsened by forward purchase contracts made just as raw material prices peaked. The review of purchasing and supplies would include the following headings:

- Organization and control of the purchasing.

- An assessment of the effectiveness of the buying department.

- Principal raw materials.

- Key suppliers.

- Supplier reliability.

- Rating vs. the alternatives.

- Supplier relationships.

- Extent of dependence on suppliers.

- Terms of trade – payment, contracts, returns, lead times.

- Price volatility.

- Quality control procedures.

- Procedures for receiving, storing and issuing stock.

- The adequacy of warehousing facilities.

PRODUCTION

The focus should be on the future. Are there any constraints on capacity? Is a costly overhaul going to be needed in the near future? How well do production facilities compare with those of the competition? Are lead times under control and on a par with industry standards? Do research and production work effectively together? A full due diligence report will include:

- Key production processes and how they are organized.

- Production statistics, lead times and quality control.

- Main items of plant and equipment, age and serviceability.

- Competitiveness of the company's production capabilities in its main areas of activity.

- Capacity/growth issues. Potential bottlenecks.

- Review of planned capital expenditure.

- Impact of new technologies.

- Stockholding policy.

- Subcontracting arrangements.

- Research and development, an explanation of what R&D is carried out:
  - Is it properly controlled?
  - Is it adequate to maintain the future growth?

PROPERTY

Liaise with legal due diligence and provide details of the target's properties including:

- List of leasehold/freehold premises.

- Location.

- Form and terms of tenure.

- Current usage.

- Date of acquisition.

- Cost and current valuation.

- Planned future expenditure.

- Planned disposals/redevelopments.

- Recent valuations.

- A schedule of the net book values of the properties. (A professional open-market valuation of the properties may need to be undertaken by a firm of chartered surveyors and valuers).

- Review title documents to property.

- Obtain copies of all appraisals.

- Investigate whether there are charges or other encumbrances over property or assets.

Leasehold properties

- For leasehold property:
    – term;
    – renewal rights;
    – rent;
    – assignability.

- For any let properties details of:
    – tenants;
    – terms of lease;
    – rental income.

Are current properties sufficient to meet growth plans?

MANAGEMENT AND HUMAN RESOURCES

This section is not just about explaining and commenting on organization structure, reporting lines, and so on. A valuable by-product of FDD, which should always be requested, is the accountant's view on management. The FDD team spends a number of weeks close to management and interviews them extensively. It is better placed than most to comment on management's strengths and weaknesses. Accountants also need to take a view on the impact of other human resources issues that can be factored into past and future profitability. For example high staff turnover and low staff morale are usually the symptom of problems in a business, as could be the recent loss of good staff. In addition, labour shortages may make it impossible to achieve planned growth.

Provide details of:

- Management structure. Comment on any gaps or imbalances.

- Culture and management style.

- Directors and senior management:
  - length of service;
  - responsibilities;
  - other interests.

- Main points in service contracts.

- Pension and benefit entitlements.

- Changes in senior management in the last three–five years.

- Any proposed changes following the proposed acquisition.

- Management's strengths and weaknesses.

- Company dependence on any key individuals.

- Management succession plans/policies.

- Compliance with Cadbury and Greenbury.

Liaise with employment/legal due diligence and provide details of the workforce including:

- Terms of employment.

- Analysis of employees between:
  - different areas of the business;
  - different functions;
  - full time vs. part time.

Liaise with employment/legal due diligence and provide details on:

- Union arrangements.

- Staff turnover.

- Remuneration policies.

- Frequency of pay reviews/date of next/last pay review.

- Terms and conditions of employment.

- Any unfair dismissal or other employment related claims.

Assess the strength of the human resource management of the business.

Assess the extent to which its workforce provides a competitive advantage to the business.

Comment on availability of staff, recruitment policy and training including:

- Skill shortages.

- Use of temporary or part-time employees.

- Recruitment plans and policies.

- Training plans and policies.

Liaise with pensions/legal due diligence and give details of pension schemes and an indication of their funding position.

Summarize any important relationships with outside contractors and professional advisers and the extent of the target's reliance upon them.

ACCOUNTING POLICIES AND INFORMATION SYSTEMS

This section analyzes and assesses the key elements of the accounting and management information systems. It is fundamental to the whole financial due diligence exercise not just because of the impact the reliability of the information can have, but also because of the impact accounting policies and their interpretation can have on reported profits. Topics to be covered should include:

- A summary of accounting policies and treatments.[1]

- Whether the accounting policies and treatments comply with generally accepted accounting standards.

- An explanation of any accounting policies and treatments that are unacceptable.

- Whether, and to what extent, accounting policies and treatments are consistent with the policies adopted by the purchaser.

- Whether accounting policies and treatments have been applied consistently during the period under review.

---

1   Note: The term 'accounting policy' refers to the overall policy adopted by the company. For example stock may be valued at 'the lower of cost or net realisable value'. The 'accounting treatment' refers to the bases and assumptions used by management to apply that policy. For example a company may write down a particular line of stock if it is not sold within six months of purchase. Clearly any change of accounting policy or treatment from one year to another can result in the profit trend being distorted.

- An overview of management information systems.

- A description of the main management information reports produced by the company.

- A review and assessment of the costing systems.

- Management's assessment of whether they have sufficiently accurate and timely information to allow them to monitor and control the business and to react to any opportunities or threats.

- Management's views on the future development of systems.

- Management's opinion on the effectiveness of the information systems

- A summary of weaknesses which need to be addressed.

- Performance vs. budget since the last accounts date and the impact of any variance on the forecast for the full year.

Reporting accountants should also be asked to assess:

- The financial records produced by the target and the systems of internal control. Compare with the acquirer's policies.

- The target's costing systems and the budgetary control and forecasting systems. Is budgetary process effective? How accurate has it been historically?

- The management information produced by the target including an assessment of auditors' management letters.

COMPUTER SYSTEMS

Computer systems may be covered by IT specialists (see Checklist 13) but, if not, reporting accountants should:

- Describe the main computer systems.

- Review third party maintenance contracts.

- Report on software ownership and maintenance.

- Report on security.

- Assess backup arrangements.

- Assess the adequacy of the current systems for present and future needs.

TRADING RESULTS

This section analyzes the historical profit and loss account of the business for the last three–five years, together with the most recent management accounts. The approach is to take each category of income and:

- Break down the figures so that their composition can be understood.

- Analyze the trend in results to understand any unusual items, the relationship between the figures and any underlying patterns.

- Understand where the profits come from.

Provide a summary of the consolidated results of the target covering the last three–five years.

Break down gross profit and analyze by each main activity for the last three–five years together with an explanation of significant variations.

List adjustments to be made to the profit and loss accounts and balance sheets over the review period to reflect consistent accounting policies or the impact of exceptional items.

Analyze overhead expenses and comment on significant fluctuations.

Explain the major fluctuations in turnover and profits during the review period.

Explain and comment on trends in the results and note any exceptional profits or losses.

Assess the target's vulnerability to changes in market conditions, interest rates and any other significant factors.

BALANCE SHEET

The approach to the balance sheet section is similar to that for the profit and loss analysis, in that each significant asset and liability is examined to ensure that:

- The basis of valuation appears to be reasonable.

- There has been no distortion in the trend.

- Assets and liabilities are properly recorded. It is not unknown for crucial assets not to be owned by the business or for liabilities to have not yet crystallized.

Net assets

Provide a summary statement of the consolidated balance sheets of the target as at * date and * date.

Analyze and comment on the main assets and liabilities of the target as at * date.

Fixed assets

The aim is to assess whether the fixed assets are consistently and reasonably valued and whether they are adequate to support the projected future earnings of the company:

- Are intangible assets reasonably valued?

- What is the composition of fixed assets and how have their values been arrived at?

- Are there detailed registers and analyzes?

- Have there been any recent independent valuations?

- Are the depreciation policies reasonable and consistently applied?

- Does the company have clear title to its main assets?

- Has the company capitalized interest or own labour within fixed assets?

- What capital commitments are there?

- What capital expenditure is required?

Stock and work in progress

Relatively small errors in stock and work in progress records can significantly distort the overall trend in the results of the company. Financial due diligence should therefore comment on:

- Whether stock is valued appropriately, particularly where overheads are included. (Overheads should be classified according to whether they are a direct production cost or not. Stock valuations should be based on 'normal' activity levels.)

- How slow moving or obsolete stock is identified and provided for. (Provisions can be too low, thus inflating profits. One-off provisions can be delayed.)

- How work in progress (WIP) is valued (production problems and stock spoilages should be written off to the profit and loss account).

- How profit is recognised.

- The appropriateness of the depreciation rate.

Debtors and receivables

Review:

- The credit control procedures.

- Analyzes of aged debtors, provisions and bad debts written off for consistency and whether the making and release of provisions or the writing off or writing back of a bad debt has distorted the trend in the results.

The recoverability of debtors is important to a potential acquirer:

- Is the debtor age profile acceptable?

- What is the trend?

- Is there an acceptable system for establishing and enforcing credit terms?

- Are bad debt reserves created on a reasonable basis?

- What is the past experience with bad debts?

- Is the business vulnerable to large debtors defaulting?

Financing and bank arrangements

Show how the target finances its activities, including any special financial arrangements.

Are cash and bank accounts properly controlled?

How are bank reconciliations carried out?

What are the cheque signatory and authorisation limits?

How does the treasury function (if relevant) operate?

Creditors and other liabilities

These should be analyzed in order to identify any liabilities which have not been disclosed or any unusual items or trends:

- Does the company receive any special credit terms?

- Is the business under creditor pressure?

- Are there any long-term liabilities such as hire purchase and finance lease obligations?

- Are there any loans from shareholders that could be repayable in the short term?

- Are the liabilities reported in the latest balance sheet complete? (Every business has liabilities which are not recorded in the balance sheet and every long-term or contingent liability that is recorded involves a degree of subjectivity.)

- Are provisions properly made and appropriately calculated? For example is the warranty provision in the balance sheet in line with what might be expected from warranty terms and product performance?

Compare notes with legal due diligence and give summary details of:

- Any material long-term and/or onerous contracts.

- Banking facilities available to the target, including covenants and any onerous conditions, breaches and renewal dates.

- The target's capital structure.

CASH FLOW

The relationship between profit and cash generation is a vital piece of knowledge which FDD must report on as thoroughly as possible. There may be perfectly good reasons for differences between profit and cash. A heavy investment programme may be one, as may rapid sales growth. On the other hand, it could be down to poor cash management which, for example could manifest itself as frequent breaches of overdraft limits.

Show the target's cash flows covering the three-year period ended * date, reconcile profit and cash, and comment on the target's ability to continue to generate cash on the same basis.

SHARE CAPITAL AND RESERVES

Describe and quantify share capital and reserves during the period under review:

- Are there are any unusual reserves or restrictions on distributions to shareholders?

Explain changes to the share capital and reserves during the period under review.

Provide details of the activities of, and relationship with, any other companies owned by, or in which an interest is held by, the shareholders or directors of the target company that have a trading or other relationship with the target.

TAXATION

After discussion with taxation/legal due diligence give summary details of:

- The current position with regard to the agreement of taxation liabilities.

- Deferred taxation.

- Shortfall clearances and assessments and details of any unusual PAYE or VAT practices and the findings of the last inspection of these areas.

FINANCIAL PROJECTIONS

Review the profit and cash flow projections of the target for the period ending * date, including:

- The method of preparation.

- Arithmetical accuracy.

- The commercial assumptions made by the directors. Comment on any assumptions that appear unrealistic.

- Cash flow projections vs. borrowing facilities.

Provide a sensitivity analysis of the projections by flexing the key assumptions and taking into account the findings of commercial due diligence.

OTHER MATTERS

Discuss with legal due diligence and give summary details of:

- Any current, pending or threatened litigation or legal proceedings against or involving the target.

- Details of any contingent liabilities.

- A summary of the target's insurance cover.

Legal Due Diligence

OBJECTIVE

L egal due diligence is undertaken to achieve three objectives. These are to:

- Uncover potential liabilities.

- Find any legal or contractual obstacles (and devise ways of overcoming them).

- Provide the basis of the final agreement.

6

Legal Due Diligence

EXECUTIVE SUMMARY

Provide a short executive summary dealing with the main legal risks and opportunities in doing this deal, from the buyer's commercial point of view, along with an assessment of the likelihood of those risks materializing and the costs if they do. Summarize what warranty/indemnity protection should be negotiated, along with an indication of the priority for each point.

CORPORATE RECORDS

Determine exact corporate name and address.

Summarize the Memorandum and Articles of Association, and all amendments made by the target and each subsidiary of the target.

Verify location of certificate of incorporation and all statutory books of the target and its subsidiaries.

Summarize legal structure of the company and its subsidiaries. Provide:

- A list, with details of corporate name, address, activities, etc., of all dormant, joint venture, subsidiary, group and associate companies.

- A family tree showing the relationship between them and the ownership chain to ultimate beneficial owners.

- Details of any branch, place of business or substantial assets outside the UK.

- Details during the last six years of any:
  - incorporations;
  - acquisitions;
  - disposals;
  - windings up.

Review:

- Minutes of all Board of Director's, committee and shareholders' meetings.

- Material information or documents furnished to shareholders and to directors during the last two years.

SHARES

Determine the capitalization, and authorised and issued shares of the target and each subsidiary.

Provide a description of shares, summarize rights of each class of share capital.

Determine names of shareholders and holdings, and whether any shareholders are under any legal disability (e.g. as a result of mental illness).

Do any of the major shareholders have any interests in other businesses which could be in competition with the target?

Determine the existence of warrants, options and other rights to acquire shares.

Summarize shareholder agreements and report on their effect, if any, on the proposed transaction and, if they are to survive, the effect on any future transactions; for example agreements or other arrangements restricting the transfer or ownership of shares or the voting of shares.

Investigate whether any shares of the stock of the target or any subsidiary have been issued in violation of company law.

Report on any encumbrances over shares.

Summarize stock option, stock purchase and other employee benefit plans and agreements.

Obtain and review copies of all correspondence and other communications with shareholders.

Confirm all dividends or distributions declared, made or paid since incorporation have been declared, made or paid in accordance with the Articles and the Companies Acts.

Obtain details of any:

- Shares created or issued in the last six years.

- Other changes in share capital in the last [six] years.

- Issue of, or proposals to issue, share capital since the last year-end.

Check that those from whom the shares are to be bought legally own them and make sure that the new owner is not going to be responsible for any liabilities attaching to the shares which were entered into by the previous owners. This means:

- Inspecting documents relating to the allotment, and issue and transfer of shares, the approval of transfers at board meetings and registration of the various transfer documents.

- Checking that former shareholders have returned their certificates and that the shareholders who are selling have certificates.

DISPENSATIONS

Has the target or any group company passed a resolution to take advantage of any of the dispensations contained in the 1985 Companies Act? I.e. to dispense with:

- Accounts before an AGM?

- Annual appointment of auditors?

- Holding AGMs?

- The need to renew the duration of an authority to allot shares and debentures beyond five years?

DEBT

Investigate the indebtedness of the target and subsidiaries, including a review of loan agreements, notes, mortgages and security agreements. Include any off balance sheet financing arrangements and the use of Special Purpose Vehicles where there is recourse to the target.

Review other financing arrangements, including sale and leaseback arrangements, capital leases and hire purchases. Include any off balance sheet financing arrangements and the use of Special Purpose Vehicles where there is recourse to the target.

Report on the terms and assignability of any loan agreements.

Review correspondence with lenders and demonstrate compliance with financial covenants.

Report on any debt arrangements, guarantees or indemnification between officers, directors or shareholders and the Company.

INSOLVENCY

Has any order been made, or resolution passed, for the winding up of the target or any subsidiary?

Has any administration order been made, or any petition for such an order presented, in respect of the target or any group company?

PROPERTY

Liaise with financial due diligence and provide details of the target's properties including:

- Leasehold/freehold premises.

- Location.

- Form and terms of tenure.

- Current usage.

- Date of acquisition.

- Cost and current valuation.

- Planned future expenditure.

- Planned disposals/redevelopments.

- Recent valuations.

- A schedule of the net book values of the properties. (A professional open-market valuation of the properties may need to be undertaken by a firm of chartered surveyors and valuers.)

- Title documents to property.

- Copies of all appraisals.

- Whether there are charges or other encumbrances over property or assets.

- For leasehold property:
    - term;
    - renewal rights;
    - rent;
    - assignability.

- For any let properties details of:
  - tenants;
  - terms of lease;
  - rental income.

Are current properties sufficient to meet growth plans?

If not covered elsewhere, obtain copies of all studies, site evaluations, and governmental filings and reports prepared by consultants or employees concerning the presence of hazardous materials or toxic substances on, under or about any property owned or leased by the target or any subsidiary.

INTELLECTUAL PROPERTY (If not covered elsewhere, see also Checklist 15)

Confirm that the company's systems, software and technology are owned solely by the target and do not infringe on any other party's rights.

AGREEMENTS

Review major contracts, including contracts currently under negotiation (to be reviewed for term, appropriateness post-acquisition, assignability and any disputes).

Sales contracts.

Distribution contracts, including all agreements with independent sales representatives, distributors and franchisees.

Warranty agreements.

Supply agreements.

Employment contracts.

Union agreements.

Management contracts.

Profit share agreements.

Consulting agreements.

Licence/franchise arrangements granted by the target.

Details of all licences or consents, permits or authorities necessary to carry on business.

Partnership or joint venture agreements of any partnership in which the target or any subsidiary is a member. If any partnership is material, additional due diligence will be necessary.

Sponsorship agreements.

Pension plans.

All insurance agreements in force with respect to the target and each subsidiary.

All other material contracts. A material contract is one calling for the payment or receipt by the target or a subsidiary of more than a specified amount during any 12-month period.

Will the acquisition have any adverse effect on the trade of the target or be in breach of any contractual obligation?

EMPLOYMENT (Unless dealt with separately, see also Checklist 8)

Obtain a list of the target's officers, directors and employees earning more than a specified amount.

Obtain a schedule showing the total number of employees, their job classifications, average compensation and location of employment.

Review:

- All of the target's and subsidiaries' profit sharing, pension, retirement, deferred compensation, incentive compensation, stock option, health and welfare, and other benefit plans and all correspondence relating to such plans, including correspondence with the tax authorities and actuaries. Review actuarial reports.

- All personnel policies.

- All employment, consulting, termination, golden parachute and indemnity agreements.

- All collective bargaining and other labour agreements.

Investigate all pending litigation or administrative matters involving employees, including discrimination charges and unfair dismissal claims.

COMPLIANCE

Obtain and comment on any licences and permits, and all judgments, orders, or decrees to which the target or any subsidiary is subject.

Obtain and comment on reports or other documents filed with governmental agencies that have regulatory power over the target or a subsidiary.

Verify that licences are still in force and not about to be taken away.

Check whether the proposed acquisition would affect licences in any way.

Are there licences the target does not have which it should have?

Are licences transferable? If the target holds the licences this is not an issue. It is an issue in an assets deal or where the licences are held by another entity such as the target's parent company.

If licences are not transferable, will new licences be forthcoming?

Verify that the target has complied with statutory requirements to file documents at Companies House. In particular, have all charges on the company's assets been properly recorded and filed?

Are special accreditations critical to a target company's profitability? For example it may be accredited to test safety critical equipment. If so, is the target still conforming to the relevant standards?

LITIGATION

Provide a summary of all pending or threatened material legal actions, administrative proceedings, governmental investigations or inquiries against or involving the target or any subsidiary.

Summarize recent or pending changes in the law that might affect the target's business.

Review correspondence with customers or suppliers relating to complaints or disputes.

Analyze and comment on any disputes with suppliers, competitors or customers.

Review correspondence with auditors or accountants regarding threatened or pending litigation, assessment or claims.

Summarize and comment on any decrees, orders or judgments of courts or governmental agencies.

Review settlement documentation.

Obtain a description of any investigations pending or in progress into the affairs of the target.

ANTITRUST (Unless covered elsewhere, see also Checklist 16)

Provide a list of where antitrust filing is required and a timetable for filing in each jurisdiction.

Obtain the information required to file with each antitrust authority.

Review all covenants not to compete, confidentiality agreements, and other restrictive agreements.

Report on any anti-competitive behaviour, real and potential.

INSURANCE (Unless covered elsewhere, see also Checklist 17)

Provide a summary of, and commentary upon, all the target's material insurance policies covering property, liabilities and operations, including product liabilities and any other insurance policies in force such as 'key man' policies or director indemnification policies.

Review all other relevant documents pertaining to the company's insurance and liability exposure.

CONSENTS AND RELEASES

Are any consents or releases needed before the transaction can complete? For example a target company's shares may need release from a parent company debenture, one group of shareholders might have pre-emption rights or there might be a need to consult with the target's Works Councils or Joint Venture Partners.

Commercial Due Diligence (CDD)

OBJECTIVES

Commercial due diligence (CDD) is a mini strategy review. The objectives of CDD are to:

- Confirm the achievability and sensitivity of the business plan.

- Assess sales operations, channel structure and customer requirements.

- Test volume, growth, price, mix and margin assumptions against market realities.

- Identify the value drivers of the acquisition and confirm synergy assumptions.

- Highlight risks and opportunities.

- Provide an input to the implementation plan.

- Give recommendations on long-term strategy.

- Judge management ability against the industry.

CHECKLIST 7.1 Commercial Due Diligence (CDD) Checklist for Initial Management Meeting

Before beginning commercial due diligence (CDD), hold a meeting with the target company management to:

- Prepare a briefing on the target and its markets.

- Reassure the management team that the buyer appreciates the sensitivities involved in market investigation work and will not disrupt the target's commercial relationships.

- Obtain customer and other contact details and agree the best approach.

- Examine internal procedures.

- Open a channel of communication.

- Assess the target's market strategy.

7.1.1 Assessing the Target's Market Strategy

TRACKING AND MEETING CUSTOMER NEEDS

Ask management the following:

- What is the state of current relationships with customers?

- What are the main benefits you deliver to your customers? (They should be able to list a small number of generic benefits.)

- Do your competitors offer these benefits? (If they are truly generic the answer will be 'yes'.)

- How regularly do you monitor your performance on these benefits? (The more frequently the better.)

- Do customer satisfaction measurements influence marketing policies?

- How good are you at doing what matters to customers?

- Which of these statements best describes your company?

    1.   We are better than the competition.

    2.   We are different to the competition.

    (Being better is a more important driver of profitability than being unique.)

- What is your Unique Selliing Point (USP)? (But note, customers buy benefits, not a USP.)

- How 'front of mind' do you think you are when potential buyers are contemplating their next purchase of this type of product? (The top few suppliers in any market win a disproportionate amount of business.)

- Does the management have a shared vision of how and why customers buy your type of product, generate their list of potential providers and narrow that list down to their final selection? (They should otherwise how do they know where to focus their energies?)

- What do your competitors do really well and what are they trying to do better? (Alarm bells should ring if the target does not know.)

- What would the market beg you and your competitors to do better? (How hard is the target thinking about innovation or out performing the competition if it does not know?)

MAKING STRATEGY REALITY

Do all staff understand the customer service and quality strategy?

Does the target use customer satisfaction measurements to evaluate and reward staff?

How regularly does the target evaluate competitors' service and quality provision?

Does the target have the mechanisms and processes for management to focus on strategy?

Are they looking to the future, confronting industry changes?

MARKET CHOICES

Does management use a market definition based on customer needs and customer differences?

Do they have a model of market segmentation based on customer benefits?

Does their market segmentation link strategy to operations?

Do they know what they are looking for in markets (marketing attractiveness) and in market position?

Can they list their priority markets and segments on a single sheet of paper and justify those choices?

THE VALUE PROPOSITION

What does management view as the target's core competencies?

Are the target's core competencies the basis of their differentiation?

Does the target have a basis for competitive differentiation that is both effective and sustainable?

Can management write down the target's value proposition on half a sheet of paper? Does it look convincing?

What does the target do to help its customers achieve the following:

- Increase revenues?

- Decrease costs?

- Increase profitability?

- Better respond to the needs of their customers, to new threats or opportunities that might be presented to them?

- Improve productivity?

- Improve their cycle time?

- Improve the satisfaction, retention and growth of their customers?

- Improve quality?

- Improve the satisfaction of their employees?

7.2   A Full CDD Exercise

KEY PURCHASE CRITERIA (see Checklist 7.2.1)

Commercial due diligence enquiries take place under three headings – market, competitive position and management. The aim is to use all three to assess how the target will perform as both a standalone business and under new ownership (for example after integration).

Ask also about Key Purchase Criteria (KPCs), See Checklist 7.2.2 – Determining KPCs Step 1.

EXECUTIVE SUMMARY

Summarize the main findings, including an assessment of the trends in the target's market, its competitive position and an overall assessment of prospects for sales and gross margin, both for the target and for the combined entity (if applicable). The target's standalone prospects should be summarized in such a way that findings can be fed into the valuation model.

MARKET

Under 'market' comes four sub-analyzes:

1. The target's products/services.

2. Market size, structure and growth.

3. Customers. Who are they and what do they want?

4. Competitors. Who are they and what are their strengths and weaknesses relative to delivering the benefits sought by consumers and relative to the target?

Products/services

What are the products/services?

Is the bulk of the company's profits based on one product?

What are the distinguishing advantages of the products/services?

Do the products require special knowledge?

How important is after sales service?

Are there products which do not fit the post-acquisition strategy?

- Could these be sold?

- Should these be sold?

Are there gaps in the product range?

Could more products be added? What are the implications of doing this?

Could the products be better targeted?

Are the target's sales and distribution adequate?

What distribution strategy has the company chosen? (Exclusive, selective, etc…)

What value do distribution partners contribute to the value delivered by the target?

What is the target's value proposition to its distribution partners?

Does the product require highly skilled sales people?

If so, are the sales staff of sufficient quality?

Is the sales force sufficient for future requirements?

Is a specialist distribution network needed?

R&D

How important is innovation to the customer base?

How innovative are the target's products?

How high are R&D costs?

Does the target company create new needs?

Suppliers

Who are they?

Is the target dependent on a small number of critical products?

Is the target dependent on a small number of suppliers?

Does the target company have a good relationship with its suppliers?

What is the supply/demand balance in the supply industry? How is this likely to change?

CAPABILITIES AND RESOURCES

What are the target's capabilities and resources? (See Checklist 7.2.3.)

MARKET SIZE, STRUCTURE AND GROWTH FOR EACH PRODUCT/SERVICE

Risk: The market might not be as big as thought or not growing as quickly or may be structurally unsuited to making decent returns.

Objective: To establish the current market size and to forecast the expected growth in the segments relevant to the target.

Questions:
Describe market structure (market shares, routes to market, etc.), how the structure has changed over time and determine the drivers of change, for example technology, legislation/regulation, consolidation, globalization and impact of e-commerce and their likely impact over the next three–five years.

How do the target's markets segment? Define the market in terms of customer benefits/the role of the target's products in the value chain.

What are the substitute products/services?

What are the geographical boundaries of the market?

How large are the market segments which the target serves today?

What is the historical market growth rate?

What are the drivers of growth?

How fast are the segments growing? Quantify likely future growth (if possible in terms of volume and price).

Are there threats from substitute products, new technologies or new entrants?

Identify any complementary products and services and any alternative applications for the target's products and services.

Does the company fully exploit product/service advantages?

Does the target company influence the way clients consume?

Does the target company create new needs/is the company adding new options especially in complementary products and services?

If not, why not? Is there scope for this?

Can suppliers, regulations or other external influences change the basis of profitability in the market?

Assess market cyclicality and the impact of economic variables, for example recession, interest rates, exchange rates.

Describe and assess the relevance for the target of each of the competitive forces based on Porter's five forces analysis (barriers to entry, demand/supply balance, relative bargaining power, impact of buyer consolidation, etc.). Give an opinion on the outlook for market price levels. (See Checklist 7.2.2.)

Assess market attractiveness.

In which segments does the target have the capabilities to compete in the future?

CUSTOMERS

Risks:
That the segments served by the target are shifting.

That the benefits delivered by the product or service are, or will, be better delivered by someone else and therefore that sales volumes will decline.

That increasing customer sophistication will push the product or service to price-based competition.

Objective: To establish customers' key purchase criteria and their future buying intentions.

Questions:
Who are the target's major customers by segment?

What are their purchase criteria? What do they value?

What does the target's market offering produce in customer value, satisfaction and loyalty?

Can the target company influence these motives?

How important is the product to its buyers?

How much evaluation goes into the product purchase?/Do customers buy this product as a commodity or as something more special requiring significant input from the target?

How does the target perform relative to customers' purchase criteria?

Are there unmet needs?

Are there likely to be changes in buying behaviour?

What are customers' switching costs?

KEY PURCHASE CRITERIA (KPCs)

What are the KPCs? (See Checklist 7.2.1 for determining KPCs.)

What is the relative importance of each KPC?

How does the target and its competitors rate against each KPC?

COMPETITORS

Risk: That the target company does not have adequate resources and capabilities to survive the competition.

Objective: To assess the competition's relative strengths and weaknesses.

Questions:
Who are the major competitors?

- Ownership.

- Size.

- Summary financial information.

- Main activities.

- Customers and segments served.

- What is their degree of commitment to each market area?

- What are their main strengths and weaknesses by product/segment served?

- What are their sources of competitive advantage?

- Are there indirect competitors?

- Do the competitors control access to distribution channels?

COMPETITIVE POSITION

Risk: That the target company is outperformed in open competition.

Objective: To assess the target company's relative strengths and weaknesses.

Questions:
Describe and evaluate the target's market positioning vs. competitors.

Has the company succeeded in differentiating itself from the competition?

What is the target's product/service quality relative to the competition?

Could quality be improved?

Is there any brand loyalty? If so, what are its origins? How enduring is it?

Is the target's brand name fully exploited?

What are the strengths and weaknesses of the target's key products and services relative to the competition?

What is the supply/demand balance in the relevant market?

How well does the target perform relative to the competition? (See 'Key Purchase Criteria' above.)

- How well does the company perform relative to the KPCs? Rate the target's performance against customers' KPCs.

- Rate competitors' performance relative to customers' KPCs. Do the competitors meet the needs of customers better than the target?

To what extent is the target's market position based on differentiating capabilities which create a robust and sustainable value proposition to customers which is better than those of the competition?

Do the distinguishing advantages of the target's products/services correspond with the KPCs?

What is the degree of competitive rivalry?

Does the target avoid head-on competition?

How does the target's pricing compare with the competition's?

What is the price policy? (Maximisation of profits, of market share, etc...)

Is there scope for price increases?

Does the price cover all the costs?

In the view of the market, is the price consistent with the quality offered?

How realistic is the threat of new entrants?

MANAGEMENT

Risk: That management cannot deliver.

Objective: To assess the strengths and weaknesses and any gaps in the capabilities of the management of the target company/combined entity.

Questions:
Can management drive the things that matter through the company to the marketplace?

Can it deliver the strategy?

Typical activities:
Interviews with market participants (such as customers) and others close to the company (such as recent leavers).

Management referencing (see Checklist 9.1).

Competency-based management interviews (see Checklist 9.2).

7.2.1 Determining Key Purchase Criteria (KPCs)

STEP 1: MANAGEMENT MEETING

- Ask management to list the top five Key Purchase Criteria (KPCs) used by customers in each of their target segments or business unit (it is important to get a comprehensive list early on).

- Ask management for the relative importance of each KPC and whether it is likely to change in the future (useful for assessing future competitive position).

- Ask management to articulate their strategy (value proposition) for each of their target segments.

- Ask management to explain which Key Performance Indicators (KPIs) they use to monitor performance.

STEP 2: CUSTOMER INTERVIEWS

- In the first few interviews, ask interviewees to validate the list of KPCs offered by management (they may not be the same!) and amend as necessary.

- Ask each interviewee to give an importance weighting (on a scale of 1–5 where 5 is very important) for each of the KPCs on the list and get them to rate the performance of those competitors with which they are familiar (including the target).

CHECKLIST
7.2.2

Five Forces

Table 7.2, below, is designed to be a structured means of assessing each of the Five Forces. It is to be completed from the target's point of view. It is important to get the scoring the right way round; the higher the score the less benign the industry structure.

Table 7.2   Assessing the Five Forces

THE THREAT OF NEW ENTRANTS: BARRIERS TO ENTRY

Factor	Extent to which the factor applies Tick appropriate box (5 = low/easy, 1 = high/ very difficult)				
Score	1	2	3	4	5
What is the extent of economies of scale, if any?					
Is the experience curve important?					
What size of investment is required to reach cost parity with existing players?					
To what degree do consumers perceive products or services to be clearly differentiated? (5 = not at all, 1 = very much so)					
How big are customers' switching costs?					
To what degree is the industry regulated?					
Sub-total					

THE THREAT OF NEW ENTRANTS: ACCESS TO COST ADVANTAGES WHICH ARE INDEPENDENT OF SCALE

Factor	Ease of access Tick appropriate box (5 = low/easy, 1 = high/ very difficult)				
Score	**1**	**2**	**3**	**4**	**5**
Access to distribution channels					
Access to essential technology					
Access to raw materials					
Access to favourable locations					
Access to other cost advantages which are independent of scale					
Total					

THE THREAT OF NEW ENTRANTS: SUMMARY

Score	**1**	**2**	**3**	**4**	**5**
Grand Total					

THE BARGAINING POWER OF SUPPLIERS

Factor	Extent to which the factor applies Tick appropriate box (1 = low, 5 = high)				
Score	**1**	**2**	**3**	**4**	**5**
The degree of concentration among suppliers					
The size of suppliers relative to buyers					
The degree of substitutability between products of the various suppliers					
The amount of, and potential for, vertical integration					
The extent to which the target is important to the supplier (5 = low, 1 = high)					
How easily can the target company switch suppliers?					
Total					

CUSTOMER BARGAINING POWER

Factor	Extent to which the factor applies Tick appropriate box (1 = low, 5 = high)				
Score	**1**	**2**	**3**	**4**	**5**
The degree of concentration among customers					
The size of customers relative to the target					
How easy is it for customers to substitute between products of their suppliers and potential suppliers?					
The ease with which customers can switch suppliers (5 = easy, 1 = difficult)					
The amount of, and potential for, vertical integration by customers					
The costs/practicability of customers switching suppliers					
Sub-total					
	Extent to which the factor applies Tick appropriate box (1 = low, 5 = high				
Score	**1**	**2**	**3**	**4**	**5**
The importance to the customer of the target's product or service in terms of its cost base					
The importance to the customer target's product or service in terms of quality (1 = high, 5 = low)					
Total					

THE THREAT OF SUBSTITUTES

Factor	Extent to which the factor applies Tick appropriate box (1 = low, 5 = high)				
Score	**1**	**2**	**3**	**4**	**5**
How big is the threat of substitute products?					

INTERNAL INDUSTRY RIVALRY

Factor	Extent to which the factor applies Tick appropriate box (1 = low, 5 = high)				
Score	**1**	**2**	**3**	**4**	**5**
Relative market share (there is usually a 'U' shaped relationship between industry concentration and industry rivalry. A high concentration will not necessarily mean a high level of competition)					
Importance of the product to the main competitors					
Extent to which the objectives of the main competitors are driven by turnover and market share					
'Normal year' supply/demand balance					
Number of competitors					
Industry growth (5 = low because low growth makes pursuit of market share more likely)					
Degree of industry differentiation (5 = low because low differentiation means a higher propensity to price wars)					
Fixed costs relative to variable costs (the higher the relative fixed costs the higher is industry sensitivity to volume around break even)					
Stage of industry cycle (1 = peak, 5 = trough)					
Height of industry exit barriers					
Total					

SUMMARY

Force	Extent to which the force applies (enter scores)				
Score	**1**	**2**	**3**	**4**	**5**
The threat of new entrants					
The bargaining power of suppliers					
Customer bargaining power					
The threat of substitutes					
Internal industry rivalry					
Total					

7.2.3 Resources and Capabilities

Is the target as profitable as its competitors?

What does it take to be successful in this industry?

Why are some firms more successful than others?

What resources and capabilities is their success based on? (See Checklist below.)

What are the stages of the value chain?

What capabilities are needed at each stage?

What resources are these capabilities based on?

TECHNOLOGY RELATED

Research expertise.

Product innovation capability.

Expertise in a given technology.

Use of IT/Internet.

Patent protection.

MANUFACTURING RELATED

Low-cost production.

Quality of manufacture.

High use of fixed assets.

Low-cost plant locations.

High labour productivity.

Low-cost product design.

Manufacturing flexibility.

DISTRIBUTION RELATED

Strong network of wholesalers/dealers.

Getting shelf space.

Fast delivery.

MARKETING RELATED

Fast, accurate technical assistance.

Courteous customer service.

Accuracy of order fulfilment.

Completeness of order fulfilment.

Timeliness of order fulfilment.

Breadth of product line.

Merchandising skills.

Product styling.

Guarantees.

Advertising.

SKILLS RELATED

Superior workforce.

Better quality control.

Design expertise.

Development expertise.

Expertise in vital technologies.

Speed in bringing new products to market.

ORGANIZATIONAL CAPABILITY

Superior information systems.

Flexibility to change with market conditions.

Management.

Workforce.

Human Resources Due Diligence

The aim of human resources (HR) due diligence is to understand the culture of the business and its employees so that the buyer can take a decision on whether to proceed with the transaction, estimate the costs and avoid the risks of proceeding, and gather the information necessary to decide how best to manage the business once the deal is done

Human resources due diligence is often presented from a legal angle. As there is so much relevant legislation, it is advisable to check that the business is complying. However, the legal issues are by no means all that need to be covered.

OBJECTIVES

The primary objectives of HR due diligence are to:

- Uncover liabilities which should be brought to the negotiating table.

- Assess their potential costs and risks and the strategy required to contain them.

- Identify and prioritize the HR issues that need to be dealt with post-acquisition.

8

Human Resources Due Diligence

EXECUTIVE SUMMARY

Summarize the main commercial issues arising from the human resources investigation. This might include the costs of complying with regulations, rationalization costs, the costs of integrating two workforces, the essentials of post-acquisition rationalization, the costs and dangers of inheriting certain union agreements or trying to merge two different cultures. Advise on warranties, indemnities and any other protection required.

EMPLOYEE INFORMATION

Obtain and analyze a full list of all employees, by process/function:

- Dates of birth.

- Dates of commencement of employment.

- Notice periods.

Obtain and review lists of:

- Part-time employees.

- Disabled employees.

- Employees on sick leave, maternity leave or secondment.

- Employees employed on fixed-term contracts.

- Employees employed on temporary and casual contracts.

- People employed as contractors.

- Any consultants or other people such as agents who provide regular services.

Deal issues

- Is the business overstaffed?

- Is the business complying with legislation relating to part-time and disabled employees?

- Are there critical areas of the business in the hands of contractors? This could throw up intellectual property issues or leave the target open to significant tax liabilities.

Integration issues

Basic employee information, dates of birth, length of service, etc. will give a profile of the workforce and allow you to come to a view on issues such as:

- Possible redundancy costs.

- Basic attitudes/how readily the workforce is likely to accept change.

- Adequacy of the workforce. How skilled is it compared with what you want post-deal? Are there training issues?

- To what extent is the business reliant upon contractors and fixed-term and casual employees? Is this likely to cause a problem?

- Are the rights of fixed-term employees likely to cause difficulties?

- Who is on maternity leave or secondment? How is their return going to be handled?

PAYROLL INFORMATION

Document, review and summarize remuneration packages, including:

- pay;
- benefits;
- bonus schemes;
- pension schemes;
- profit sharing plans.

Document and summarize:

- Planned retirements.
- Relocations in progress.
- Details of anyone receiving less than the minimum wage.

- Outstanding leaves of absence.

- Status of pension planning.

Deal issues

- Are there any hidden liabilities? For example are benefits amassed throughout the year, such as bonuses or holiday pay, properly accrued for? Are there discretionary bonuses? Discretionary bonuses are not always as 'discretionary' as might be imagined.

- Is anyone paid less than the statutory minimum wage?

- Are there any discriminatory pay structures such as different pay for men and women doing the same job or different pension arrangements or other benefits for full-time and part-time workers?

- Are employees paid a reasonable amount or will they need an increase to bring them up to the going rate?

- Are bonuses and incentives adequate?

Integration issues

- Are pay, terms and conditions, and perks, such as the company car scheme, broadly in line or will changes in terms and conditions have to be made on integration?

- Will any bonus or incentive schemes (e.g. share options) fit in on integration?

STAFF STRUCTURE

Summarize management levels and staff grading system.

Integration issues

- Who are the key workers? As there may be a high degree of dependence on a person who is not particularly high up or high profile some probing may be called for.

- What are the overlaps between acquired and existing employees? What is the relative importance and performance of acquired employees compared with existing employees? This can be extremely difficult to gauge without access to employees. Such access is rare even in agreed acquisitions.

TERMS AND CONDITIONS

Document, review and summarize:

- Standard service agreements and terms and conditions:
  - Any exceptions to the above.
  - Any promised changes to the above (including pending pay increases).
- Agency contracts.
- Staff manuals.
- Restrictive covenants and confidentiality provisions.
- Details of employees' average weekly hours.
- Employees who have opted out of the Working Time Regulations.
- Any arrangements to be followed in the event of redundancies.
- Holiday pay arrangements.
- 'Golden parachutes'.

Deal issues

- Are there any enhanced redundancy costs or golden parachutes? How much will these cost?
- Are there any unusual terms and conditions?
- Are there any discriminatory or illegal terms and conditions?
- Have any contractually binding promises been made about terms and conditions once the transaction completes?

Integration issues

- Are there any gaps or weaknesses in employment contracts? Do they need updating in the light of legislation or to address inconsistencies?
- Are there any restrictive covenants in place? Are they adequate and will they work?

INDUSTRIAL RELATIONS

Obtain and review details of:

- Dismissals, including redundancies in the last six months.

- Disciplinary and grievance procedures and all recent instances of their use.

- Disputes and litigation (past, present, threatened and pending) and not just limited to employment tribunal proceedings.

- Sickness records.

- Union membership.

- Union recognition.

- Collective agreements.

- Employee representatives, who they are and who they represent, terms of office, etc.

Deal issues

- Union representation could be a deal issue or an integration issue. Buying a business with strong union representation could mean compulsory recognition across the entire combined business.

- Examine the sickness and disability records for trends very carefully – and marry these up with insurance. You are unlikely to find anything quite as horrific or expensive as asbestos-related illnesses these days, but you never know.

- What consultative bodies are in place and do they comply with legislation? Are these sufficient for any consultation that may be required as part of the deal or are there gaps which need filling?

- Are there any claims likely against the company (past, present and future)? Will they transfer? If so, what indemnities are required?

Integration issues

- What is the standard agreed redundancy procedure in the target? For example there may be agreed ways of selecting people to be made redundant or there may be enhanced redundancy terms.

- The industrial relations history is a valuable part of piecing together a profile of the workforce. The extent to which grievance procedures have been used is a good indication of inherent problems in the business.

- Ditto the health and safety record. Look at the accident book. What is the health and safety record like?

RELATIONS WITH STATUTORY BODIES

Report on any correspondence with:

- Equality and Human Rights Commission (covers racial equality, disability rights and equal opportunities).

- The Data Protection Commissioner.

- Any health and safety Authority.

- The Inland Revenue.

Deal issues

- Health and safety is an area where legislation has pushed more responsibility onto companies. Due diligence should review the target's compliance with the legislation and if possible health and safety specialists should inspect the site. Injuries lead to claims and can also lead to the need for an expensive upgrading of worker protection. In some cases, inspectors have ordered critical equipment to be shut down with potentially very expensive consequences.

LEGAL

Document, review and summarize:

- Consulting agreements.

- Employee handbooks.

- Internal investigations/corrective actions.

- Status of personnel files.

CORPORATE CULTURE

How do the corporate cultures compare? For example:

- 'Hard-driving' vs. 'Laid back'?

- 'Patch it quick' vs. 'Do it right'?

- 'Anything for a sale' vs. 'Maintain quality/standards at all costs'?

- Technology-driven vs. marketing-driven vs. sales-driven vs. product development strategy?

- Managers vs. leaders?

How formal are the relationships across levels of management?

What are the working hours (usual and when working to deadlines)?

What is the dress code?

What perks are provided (coffee, snacks, parties, meals when working to deadlines, etc.)?

How do the following compare:

- Compensation?

- Salaries?

- Cash bonuses?

- Stock options?

Management Due Diligence

The management of a business post-merger or acquisition is critical, so much so that most private equity investors' investment decisions are driven by confidence in management.

OBJECTIVE

Management due diligence seeks to give an objective assessment of senior managers' capability both individually and collectively using disciplined methods to evaluate management, both as individuals and as a team.

For individuals:

- Profile individuals' capabilities against a broad range of general management competencies (see Checklist 9.2).

- Match these against the managerial challenges that will need to be addressed over the next few years.

- Highlight individuals' strengths and weaknesses.

- Benchmark against senior managers in other organizations.

- Indicate what areas of development or support would compensate for any weaknesses.

For the team, or proposed team, provide a profile of the senior management team which:

- Maps out the overall strengths and weaknesses of the management team as a whole.

- Identifies where individuals' strengths complement each other.

- Exposes any specific experience or capability that may be lacking in the team.

Before beginning, it must be clear what skills, resources and experience are needed for the acquisition to be successful (see Checklist 9.2).

CHECKLIST 9.1 Management Due Diligence

Table 9.1 **Identify action to be taken for key managers and key groups**

	Impact of loss	Message to deliver	Date message delivered	Person responsible	Follow up required
Key individuals					
• Name 1					
• Name 2					
• Etc.					
Key groups					

Get comfort on the background and integrity of management by reviewing CVs, job evaluations and anything else written by or about the managers being examined. Expand and verify the information contained in the CVs through a mixture of desk and primary research:

- Address. Confirmation that the manager lives at the address claimed. Brief assessment of the residence.

- Credit. Any county court judgments or other bad credit associated with either the person or the address?

- Media checks. Are there any past articles which may cause concern?

- Are the qualifications and job/education history accurate? Past experience check. Interviews with previous employers to confirm:

      – Information on the CV (dates, remuneration, responsibilities etc.).

      – Reasons for leaving.

      – Past performance? Is this as claimed?

      – How honest are they? What is their reputation as far as integrity is concerned?

      – What is central to their motivation? What makes them perform?

      – Where do they want to go?

- Verification of professional memberships.

- Industry enquiries. To try to establish whether there is anything in the manager's background which might cause concern. Is the individual seen as competent, honest and respected? Ex-colleagues make particularly revealing sources.

- A list of current directorships and shareholdings.

Undertake past-orientated, fact-based, structured, competency interviews to gather data on past performance. Start at the beginning of the candidate's career and work through to the latest job. Questions for each of the different positions held will be of the type listed in Checklist 9.3. The theory is that the past is the best predictor of the future.

Seek references. These are discussions with people who have seen the manager in action. Current and former colleagues, 360-degree feedback sessions, analysts, investors, advisers, customers and suppliers are the most obvious sources.

Consider using work samples. Work samples are answers to hypothetical 'what-if' type questions, such as 'how would you manage the integration of these two companies?'

Consider observing the management team in action and so observe the quality of their interactions and of their relationships with each other. This involves shadowing managers for a day.

REPORTING

Summarize:

- Target's organization chart and division of responsibilities.

- Strengths and weaknesses of the management team.

Give recommendations on:

- The most appropriate final organizational structure.

- The most appropriate interim organizational structure.

- Which individuals should be in which position.

Management Competencies

The five main subject headings below form a framework of competencies against which to assess management in either interviews or tests (or both).

INDIVIDUAL COMPETENCES

Flexibility. The ability to change direction or modify the way in which the individual does things. Flexibility would include a willingness to try, adaptability and a positive outlook.

Decisiveness. This is the readiness to take decisions and to act, that is, coming to conclusions and taking appropriate action.

Tenacity. The ability to stick with a problem until it is solved (and to recognise when there is no solution).

Independence. The willingness to question the accepted way of doing things.

Risk taking. The extent to which a manager is prepared to take calculated risks.

Integrity. The recognition and maintenance of high personal standards and the implementation of appropriate moral and ethical norms.

INTERPERSONAL COMPETENCIES

Communication. The ability to convey information clearly, both orally and in writing. The ability to listen.

Impact. The ability to create a favourable first impression.

Persuasiveness. The ability to persuade and influence others.

Personal awareness. The awareness of other people and of the need to take into account their thoughts and feelings before acting.

Teamwork. Contributing in an active and cooperative way with the rest of the team. Supporting others. Making decisions by consensus.

Openness. The ability to take constructive criticism. The ability to build on the contributions of other people.

ANALYTICAL COMPETENCES

Innovation. The ability to come up with imaginative and practical solutions to problems.

Analytical skills. The ability to break problems down and work on them sequentially.

Numerical problem solving. The ability to understand and analyze numerical information.

Problem solving. The ability to evaluate a situation and come to with solutions which meet customers' needs.

Practical learning. Being able to absorb, learn and apply new methods.

Detail consciousness. The ability to process large amounts of complex information.

MANAGERIAL COMPETENCIES

Leadership. The ability to guide the actions of, and achieve results through, other people.

Empowerment. The concern for developing other people and allowing them freedom of manoeuvre.

Strategic planning. The ability to hover above the day-to-day detail and see the bigger picture.

Corporate sensitivity. An understanding of where the business is going.

Project management. The ability to define the requirements of a project and lead a group towards its satisfactory completion.

Management control. The appreciation of how a business needs to be controlled and subordinates organized.

MOTIVATIONAL COMPETENCIES

Resilience. The ability to 'bounce back' when things are not going to plan.

Energy. Otherwise known as stamina and drive.

Motivation. The ability to motivate self and others.

Achievement orientation. The drive to set challenging targets and the drive to meet them.

Initiative. The ability to spot and solve problems before they arise and to act on opportunities when they present themselves.

Quality focus. The commitment to getting a job done well.

9.3 Competency-based Interviewing

Competency-based interviewing seeks to use past performance as a guide to the future. The interviewer must therefore gather evidence from specific examples from the interviewee's career. The structure for each example should be as follows.

SITUATION

What was the situation or task?

Describe the circumstances.

What was your responsibility?

Who else was involved?

ACTIONS

What happened?

What did you specifically do/say?

What problems were there?

How did you handle these problems?

EFFECT

What was the effect/outcome?

What impact did that have?

How did you measure your success?

What lessons have you learnt?

Pensions Due Diligence

Detailed due diligence will be required if the purchaser is acquiring the pension scheme(s) as part of the transaction. Purchasers will not want to have to make large, one-off contributions to the scheme(s). The objectives of pensions due diligence depend on the nature of the transaction. There are three different types of transaction to consider:

1. Purchase of an entire company.

2. Purchase of a company which is part of a larger group and participates in a group pension scheme.

3. Purchase of assets.

Any joint ventures may bring further complications.

OBJECTIVES – PURCHASE OF AN ENTIRE COMPANY

When buying a UK company in its entirety, the chances are that the workforce will come with its own pension scheme. The purchaser, therefore, needs to determine whether the scheme:

Is adequately funded?

Meets the expectations of the workforce. As a minimum, expectations will be set out in employment contracts.

Contains any 'hidden' costs. Hidden costs can arise for a number or reasons. If, for example the buyer's intention is to wind up the existing scheme and bring the acquired workforce into a new scheme there may be 'switching costs' where insured schemes are concerned.

OBJECTIVES – PURCHASE OF A SUBSIDIARY/ASSETS

If a buyer is inviting the acquired employees to join an existing scheme, or is setting up a new one on their behalf, it is common for a bulk transfer of funds to be agreed by actuaries acting for each side. They will usually agree on one of three bases:

1.   Cash equivalent amount.

2.   Past service reserve (which takes into account future salary increases).

3.   Share of the fund. Where a company is being transferred out of a group the rules may allow a share of the group fund to be transferred, rather than just a package of transfer values.

In an assets deal, if the previous employer provided employees with membership of an occupational pension scheme, the new employer must, under TUPE regulations, provide some form of pension for them. This does not have to be the same as their previous scheme but it does have to meet certain minimum standards:

The new employer must do one of the following:

*   Ensure transferring employees can join a salary-related scheme which meets certain minimum standards (a 1/80 pension payable at 65) or to which the employer contributes.

*   Ensure they can join a money purchase scheme to which the employer contributes.

*   Make contributions to a stakeholder scheme.

The minimum level of employer contributions for a salary-related scheme is 6 per cent of pensionable pay. The new employer will be expected to match employee contributions to money purchase or stakeholder schemes up to a maximum of 6 per cent of earnings each year.

Pensions Due Diligence

EXECUTIVE SUMMARY

Summary of the funding position. Recommendations on warranties. Recommendations for future pension provision.

PENSION SCHEMES

Obtain

A full list of those transferring along with details of age, pay and length of service, and contracts of employment.

Commentary on changes planned in the context of the proposed acquisition.

A copy of the target's accounts.

For each scheme from which employees are transferring:

- The Trust Deed and Rules.

- Members' handbook.

- Announcements made since both of the above were last updated.

- Confirmation that equal pay and increases are provided for.

- The latest scheme accounts.

- Latest actuarial report/review.

- Information on any unfunded pension commitments, both approved and unapproved.

Verification that Revenue Contributions Agency (CA) approval, etc. has been obtained.

Confirmation that there is no Occupational Pensions Regulatory Authority (OPRA) interest.

Taxation Due Diligence

Anglo-Saxon practice is for there to be a tax indemnity, often referred to as the tax deed. The effect is to make the seller liable for any pre-deal tax which falls due after the deal is done. In practice, indemnities are not fail-safe. Buyers carry out tax due diligence so that they know where the risks and vulnerabilities are, some of which may fall due outside of a time limited indemnity, some of which arise as a result of the transaction itself and some of which may need protection over and above the tax deed.

OBJECTIVES

The objectives of tax due diligence are fourfold:

1. To find and protect against tax exposures which are not reflected in the purchase price. This means identifying and evaluating tax liabilities for which there are no provisions.

2. To identify and plan for tax liabilities that will be triggered as a result of the transaction. The seller's indemnity will not normally cover these.

3. To structure the deal in the most tax efficient manner.

4. To ensure that post-completion integration is carried out in the most tax efficient manner subject to commercial objectives.

TAXES TO COVER

The principal taxes to be considered are:

- Corporate taxes.
- VAT/sales taxes.

- Employment taxes, such as income tax – known as Pay As you Earn (PAYE) in the UK – national insurance/health care taxes (NHI in the UK), payroll taxes and deductions.

- Employee benefit reporting.

- Stamp duties, transfer duties and capital duties on the acquisition.

The target's shareholders' personal taxes may also be of interest, especially those which may be charged to the target company, such as inheritance taxes, estate duties and gift taxes.

If the transaction is an assets deal, only stamp duty and VAT will be relevant. As these are both levied on the transaction itself, they are easily identified. A share deal, on the other hand, means taking over the company's tax affairs and tax due diligence will cover most of the taxes mentioned above.

ACTIVITIES

The main activities involved can be summarized as follows:

- Review of corporate tax returns and computations.

- Review of correspondence with tax authorities and the status of agreements on outstanding computations.

- Details of any inland revenue investigations and of tax audits by foreign tax authorities.

- Analysis of corporate tax and deferred tax provisions in financial statements.

- Review of quarterly payment procedures.

11

Taxation Due Diligence

EXECUTIVE SUMMARY

Provide an overall assessment of the buyer's exposure to any past tax liabilities, the transactional risks and the likelihood of them crystallizing, and advise on any tax planning opportunities. Give appropriate recommendations.

ACCOUNTS

Summarize tax provisions for the last [X] years.

Obtain/perform reconciliations of the tax charge shown in the accounts to the prevailing statutory rates. Investigate reasons for significant differences.

Describe deferred tax provisioning policy, verify closing balance sheet provision.

CORPORATION TAX

Obtain copies of computations, returns, assessments and correspondence with the Inland Revenue for the last [X] years.

Document status of the above.

Review filing of returns and quarterly payment compliance. A company's compliance record is a good guide to how it will be treated by the tax authorities. A poor record means that every submission will be closely examined.

Describe significant areas of correspondence with the Inland Revenue. Buyers need to be satisfied that there are no significant disputes with the tax authorities. The most common areas are capital allowance claims and bad debt provisions, un-agreed valuations (which could have an impact on capital gains liabilities) and, for international businesses, outstanding transfer pricing disputes. Buyers should also ensure that claims and elections are made within statutory time limits. Time limits could easily expire while the deal is being negotiated. Often special agreements are made with the tax authorities and it is important to understand what these are and whether they will continue.

Identify any concessionary tax treatments being followed.

Detail items still unresolved and under negotiation, quantify amounts and likely risk.

Compare above with accounts provisions. Are provisions adequate?

Summarize carry forward tax assets.

Confirm extent to which tax assets have been agreed with Inland Revenue.

Assess extent to which above tax assets are vulnerable to:

- Anti-avoidance measures.

- Not being available to the purchaser for other reasons.

Confirm and document the tax base cost of significant assets.

Summarize any past rollover/holdover claims that impact on tax base cost of significant assets.

Obtain copies of Industrial Buildings Allowance history.

Confirm all relevant elections have been validly made on time.

Review intra-group assets transfers.

Confirm group matters, for example group income election.

Obtain copies of all tax clearances sought/received. Certain clearances may be needed for the transaction to go ahead. The purchaser should make sure they have been applied for and have been properly drafted.

Review the status and outcome of overseas tax audits.

Assess overseas subsidiaries for Controlled Foreign Companies Legislation.

Obtain copies of transfer pricing policy. Review and comment on practice. Transfer pricing is almost impossible to get right and therefore an area of significant risk in cross-border acquisitions. Due diligence should determine the target's exposure to transfer pricing adjustments and any likely tax liabilities.

If the target is a member of a group:

- Are there inter-group transfers which give rise to de-grouping charges on capital gains once the deal is done?

- Understand the system for group and consortium relief surrenders and whether any payments are outstanding. Individual companies that are part of a group often do not bother to pay each other.

- Is the target liable for any taxes of the group companies not acquired?

PAYROLL TAXES

Review forms P11D.

Discuss arrangements for expenses, benefits, casual payments, etc. and check to P11Ds.

Review correspondence in respect of most recent PAYE/NIC audits.

Critically review any 'consultancy' and 'contractor' arrangements for employee status. If contractors are paid on invoice with no deductions for income tax and national insurance, what mechanisms are in place to ensure that the target has no tax liability?

Identify any share options/incentive arrangements and review for compliance/exposure for PAYE and NIC. Has the Revenue approved any profit-related pay schemes? How will they be affected by the transaction?

Obtain copies of any P11D dispensations.

Reconcile balance sheet provision for PAYE/NIC to month-/year-end returns.

Review for overseas payroll exposures, for example seconded employees etc.

Assess major risk areas. Have the relevant taxes been correctly deducted and paid over on time? Have year-end returns been correctly filed, especially benefits in kind?

VAT/CUSTOMS

Review workings supporting the last [X] years' VAT returns.

Confirm VAT status.

Document any special arrangements and compliance with them.

Review correspondence in respect of most recent audit inspection.

Confirm payments are up to date, returns up to date, no default surcharge notices.

Discuss and review procedures for:

- discounts;

- disposals of assets;

- miscellaneous sources of income;

- bad debts;

- non-deductible items.

Review and document arrangements for Customs duties.

Assess risk areas.

Consider the VAT treatment of the transaction itself.

PREVIOUS RE-ORGANIZATIONS/TRANSACTIONS UNDERTAKEN BY TARGET

Obtain details of past M&A transactions involving the target.

Review clearances.

Review due diligence.

Review warranties and indemnities.

Summarize implications for current transaction. Is there a risk of crystallization if the target has given or received tax warranties and indemnities in past M&A transactions?

TRANSACTION, STRUCTURING AND INTEGRATION ISSUES

Identify potential warranty/indemnity issues.

Advise on stamp duty.

Assess the impact of the transaction on:

- Losses and other reliefs carried forward.

- Option schemes, PRP schemes, etc.

- The vendor's tax planning.

Report on tax issues to be considered during integration planning.

Summarize any tax planning issues to be taken into account when structuring the transaction.

Structuring

Are there any post-acquisition structuring opportunities?

- Avoiding double taxation.

- Maximizing relief for interest on borrowed funds.

- Minimizing withholding taxes.

- Obtaining a step-up of assets for depreciation purposes.

- Obtaining relief for acquisition costs.

Environmental Due Diligence

OBJECTIVES

Environmental due diligence has two strands. These are identifying and quantifying:

1. Environmental risks which would be inherited such as a potential liability for cleaning up contaminated land.

2. The costs of meeting any continuing obligations, for example upgrading equipment and procedures.

PROCESS

Environmental due diligence is a two-stage process:

*   Phase 1 review, which is a review of existing knowledge, public data and other information on the target to identify any areas of concern.

*   Phase 2 review, the intrusive enquiries required to monitor, sample and fully analyze any concerns raised in Phase 1.

12

Environmental Due Diligence

PHASE 1

Undertake desk research to assess the chances of the land or surrounding area being contaminated, including the physical characteristics of the area, the hydrology and geology.

Review data rooms for:

* Environmental consultants' reports.

* Environmental policies.

* Lists of any hazardous materials kept on site.

* Details of accidents and spillages.

* Details of breaches of consents.

* Enforcement notices (following environmental damage or breach of compliance).

Review management information systems to determine whether the target is employing a formal system for environmental management, such as one based on ISO 14001, proving that it is aware of the risks its operations pose to the environment and that it has the controls in place.

Collect from the regulatory authorities information that is in the public domain, for example authorizations, permits and licences, and details of any enforcements.

Undertake selected sites visits. For those sites where a visit is justified, the objective is to see the site and see how operations are carried out. The environmental auditor will aim to:

* Further assess the nature and extent of any contamination.

- Audit the presence of substances which may cause contamination in future.

- Understand the degree of compliance with environmental regulations.

- Audit environmental management.

Reporting

Provide a report which gives a description of:

- The previous uses of the site(s) and the previous occupiers of the sites during the last 40 years and, where ascertainable, during the last 100 years.

- The present use or uses of the site(s), including details of any deposit, storage, disposal and treatment of waste or sewage.

- Manufacturing and other processes and operations, abstractions of water, mining operations, discharge of use of chemicals and any other substances.

- The geological and hydro-geological features of the site and of land within 1000 metres of the site, including the potential migration or pathways of any pollutants or contaminants from the site.

Provide a report which gives details of:

- Any plant and operating processes.

- The condition or use of any neighbouring land.

- The location of any asbestos, PCBs or formaldehyde.

- The drainage system.

- The measures for containment and prevention or pollution.

- Environmental permits and whether they are in full force and effect.

- Any works or other expenditure required within the next five years to maintain compliance with environmental standards, the presence or former presence of any underground or surface storage tanks.

- Any previous audits, assessments or other reports.

- Any actual or threatened prosecutions or civil proceedings.

- Corporate environmental policies.

Provide an assessment of:

- How management has dealt with the issues identified including an assessment of their environmental performance against statutory and/or corporate standards.

- Inefficiencies in current practices.

- Non-compliance issues.

- Steps required to rectify any concerns, non-compliances, etc.

- Priorities for environmental improvements.

- Current and future requirements.

- A possible means of achieving these improvements, together with costs and timescales.

- The extent to which the above costs have already been accounted for, for example through provisions or insurance.

- Indemnities needed.

- Any other potential risks and the chances of them crystallizing.

- Costings for any remediation works.

Describe the issues identified, for example:

- Legal and/or policy requirements.

- Areas of significantly bad environmental performance.

Give recommendations for Phase 2 audit, if any.

Highlight any ethical issues.

PHASE 2

Phase 2 is about soil and groundwater contamination. The objective is to quantify the risks from contamination generated within the site or which has come from adjoining sites and will involve sampling the soil and groundwater and analyzing the samples in a laboratory.

IT Due Diligence

OBJECTIVE

IT due diligence investigations should take place on three levels:

1. The 'audit' level. What equipment and software is there? Is it secure? Does it work? Who owns it? What are the outstanding commitments?

2. The 'management' level. How well does IT and technology support the business?

3. The 'strategic' level. Is the technology and IT organization sufficient for the future?

13 IT Due Diligence

EXECUTIVE SUMMARY

Provide a summary of the target's IT equipment and software and report on its security, functionality, ownership and any outstanding commitments. Assess the degree to which IT and technology supports the business on a day-to-day basis and make recommendations for any changes. Assess the sufficiency of the IT resources for the future and make recommendations for any changes. Give recommendations on the most appropriate and cost-effective IT organization once the transaction is complete, including costings and timetables. Assess the current IT and technical staff both as individuals and as a team.

AUDIT THE CURRENT IT SYSTEMS

Assess the vulnerability, trust and complexity of the current systems as follows:

* Vulnerability – Test the controls around physical and electronic access including unauthorized access from public networks.

* Trust – Assess the level of trust one can have based on past security failures and robustness of employee vetting procedures.

* Complexity – What is the degree of risk brought on by the complexity of the system?

What is the extent of interdependencies, that is to what extent is the system dependent on the functioning of discrete sub-systems?

How much risk is there because of reliance on a single system?

Assess:

* The degree of dependence on a small number of key people.

- The quality of system documentation.

- The level of technology.

- The degree of equipment obsolescence.

Is ownership, particularly of software, inside or outside the target company?

How dependent are the systems on a few key IT staff?

Is dependency risk likely to be compounded by any negative feelings the target's key staff may have towards the buyer or their new roles?

Assess other risks:

- The quality of system documentation. How well is the system documented? How up to date is the documentation?

- What is the degree of technology risk? Up to a point, the longer the technology has been in place, the lower the technology risk.

- What is the degree of equipment obsolescence? Will major parts of the system have to be replaced shortly after acquisition, with all the cost and uncertainty that entails?

- Is the software being used customized for the target company?

- Who are the key software vendors?

- Are the key software vendors sizeable operations and financially stable? What is the size of their installed bases? (The bigger the better.)

Does the company own the IT assets it operates?

Is the target company the licensor? If not, who is?

For how much longer are the licences valid?

Are there any limitations on licensed software? For example equipment on which it can be used, locations at which it can be used, number of users?

If existing limitations are not satisfactory, can they be extended and, if so, at what cost?

Is the licence for source code or object code?

If it is for object code, what guarantees are in place?

Will the licensor maintain the software and provide support within acceptable time limits?

Does the licensee get access to source codes if the licensor goes out of business?

If the licence is for source codes, does the target have an obligation to maintain the software itself or can this be outsourced?

Will restrictions in the software licences prevent the target outsourcing its IT function?

Review copies of all software licences and other agreements for the use and maintenance of computer systems and computer software.

MANAGEMENT LEVEL

Users' perceptions of the IT department

Does the present system support departmental and company objectives? What do the business units and functional heads say about the IT department? Where is IT rated on the following spectrum:

- Strong differentiator.
- An important element of competitive advantage.
- A necessary evil.
- A positive hindrance to progress.

How interlinked is IT with the wider business? Perceptions of:

- skill base;
- technical skills;
- team spirit;
- leadership;
- management.

Business processes

Assess the effectiveness of:

- departmental structure;
- policies and procedures;
- project management;
- QA process;
- documentation;
- training.

Is the IT organization and its business processes equal to what might be expected of it?

- Views on responsiveness.

- Is the team business-driven or technology-driven?

- At what level in the target's hierarchy is the IT department represented?

Strategic level

- How closely is the IT plan aligned with the overall corporate plan?

- What is the timescale (benefits from IT projects should be delivered in months not years)?

- How is IT helping the target's ability to respond to rapidly changing circumstances?

- How is IT giving customers added value?

- Are there well-developed plans for future development?

- Do these support the business plan?

Technical Due Diligence

OBJECTIVE

The objectives of technical due diligence are to ensure that:

- The product performs as far as buyers are concerned.

- Modifications and new features are properly identified and prioritized.

- The future, in terms of development procedures, key people and intellectual property protection, has been adequately catered for.

CHECKLIST 14 Technical Due Diligence

PRODUCT

Conduct a telephone poll of all customers who purchased each product recently. Select the customers randomly from invoices.

Conduct a telephone poll of random customers that have used the product for over a year.

Review complaint letters. Call the customers who wrote those letters.

Call any customers who wanted their money back.

Get a recent lost sales report. Call customers who selected competitive products.

How often is each product updated? What triggers a new product release? For example new features or bug fixes?

How are new features determined/prioritized?

What is the number and severity of bugs logged against each product?

Does the bug list adequately reflect the defects reported during the telephone poll?

DEVELOPMENT GROUP

Is the Development Group appropriately staffed? Quantity? Quality?

Is the Development Group supplied with adequate development equipment?

Are the development processes appropriately documented?

Are the products appropriately documented?

Is the design documentation adequate?

Has it been updated to reflect design changes and enhancements?

TECHNICAL SUPPORT GROUP

Conduct a telephone poll of customers who called technical support recently.

Conduct a telephone poll of random customers.

Is the Technical Support Group appropriately staffed?

Is the Technical Support Group supplied with adequate test equipment?

Is the Technical Support Group adequately documented?

Is the technical support response adequate? What hours are available?

Are inbound calls immediately directed to a technical support person or are they logged for call back? What is the average time for call backs? What is the worst case time for call backs?

What is the escalation procedure? When is the development group informed of a support issue? When is top management informed of a support issue? When is the salesman on the account informed of a support issue?

Do the Development Group and the Technical Support Group access the same fault tracking system?

Is there a computerized log?

Are reports generated to categorize the reasons for the calls? Call duration? Whether call back needed? How many calls to resolve the issue?

Is escalation to a second level technical support or to development?

How are emergency fixes handled? How delivered? How tracked? How integrated into next product release?

WHO IS CRITICAL TO CONTINUED SUCCESS?

Who has critical undocumented knowledge?

What is the historic employee churn?

Who is currently dissatisfied? Why?

What happens to stock options in a buyout?

Who might become dissatisfied by a buyout? Why?

Who might become too satisfied by a buyout?

INTELLECTUAL PROPERTY ISSUES

Has the product documentation, the marketing collateral, or any advertising ever inaccurately represented the capabilities of the product?

Do appropriate licences accompany all products shipped?

Does the company have full rights to any intellectual property it uses?

Did any intellectual property originate outside the company? Where? Who has rights? Are the original rights retained in the intellectual property?

Has any of the company's intellectual property ever been licensed to another entity? Is there an appropriate signed licence agreement?

Are there copyright notices in all intellectual property, documentation and disc labels?

Does the company own any patents? Are they enforceable?

Does the company infringe anyone else's patents?

Are current non-disclosure agreements in place? For employees? Contractors? Customers? Vendors? Partners?

Is the company or any employee under non-disclosure to any other entity?

Are all copies of development software and office software paid for and registered?

Does the company meet all licence agreement terms for all development software used?

Are royalties payable for any software component bundled with the company's product? Are the royalty payments current?

Intellectual Property Due Diligence

OBJECTIVE

Intellectual property is about patents, trademarks and other rights to designs and inventions. It has four strands:

1. Identification of the Intellectual Property Rights (IPRs) in a business.

2. Ownership of those rights. As the IPR necessary to carry on the business have to be transferred when the target is sold, a central concern of intellectual property due diligence is to establish that the seller owns the rights it is selling.

3. Validity. Once transferred, are those IPRs sufficient to protect the acquired company from any claims that its activities are infringing the intellectual property rights of others?

4. Uniqueness/sufficiency. Alongside the three more legal investigations outlined above, commercially a buyer would be wise to satisfy itself that the intellectual property it is buying is in fact the world-beater it thinks it is. In other words, are those IPRs sufficient to give a competitive edge?

ACTIVITIES

Intellectual property due diligence activities include the following:

*   Questions to the seller.

*   Questions to the seller's advisers – in this case lawyers and patent and trademark agents.

*   Searches in official registers, basically to verify answers to the above sets of questions.

*   Questions in and around the target company's industry.

- A review of all relevant licences, agreements and other documentation.

- A review of patent agents' correspondence and reports.

Intellectual property rights vary by territory. This means everything to do with intellectual property tends to be territorial, including:

- The rights which are recognized.

- How much, and what sort of, protection IPRs give.

- How they are acquired and registered.

- How, and for how long, they are maintained.

- What constitutes an infringement.

- Remedies available for infringements.

15 Intellectual Property Due Diligence

EXECUTIVE SUMMARY

Confirm or otherwise the existence and validity of, and title to, the intellectual property rights (IPRs) the buyer thought it was buying. Highlight any contractual protection issues. Assess the importance of IPRs in the creation and maintenance of competitive advantage.

Obtain a list of

All IPRs owned by the target which are to be transferred. Registered:

- patents;
- copyrights;
- design rights;
- registered designs;
- registered trademarks.

Not registered but are nonetheless protected by virtue of unregistered rights:

- Trademarks.
- Capable of registration, but have not been registered to maximise their protection.

Other important items that are not IPRs as such may need to be included:

- Rights to use domain names.
- Know-how/trade secrets.

All patent, trademark and design applications outstanding with an estimate of likely date of grant.

Which IPRs cover which products?

Any restrictions or limitations on the use of IPRs or third party ownership rights. Check for security interests, e.g. collateral assignments.

Obtain copies of all:

- Licences and other agreements to which the target is a party (licences can work both ways so remember the target could be a licensor or a licensee, or indeed both). Identify revenue streams or royalty obligations associated with each licence.

- Non-disclosure agreements.

Obtain details of

Any challenges to the IPRs owned, claimed, licensed or used by the target company.

Any claims that the target is infringing another company's IPRs.

Proper transfer of inventors'/authors' rights.

Arrangements to ensure that the company owns any IPRs created by work done by employees or outside parties.

The target's procedures for ensuring that IPRs are protected.

How IPRs have been enforced in the past.

All litigation involving IPRs.

Current R&D projects and an assessment of the likelihood of such projects giving rise to a patentable invention.

Payment of maintenance fees for patents and trademarks.

Employment agreements relating to IPRs. Do the agreements include non-compete clauses? Does the target remind employees of their confidentiality obligations?

Copies of all other agreements dealing with IPRs, for example rights in inventions, secrecy and non-compete agreements with research bodies such as universities and consultancies and joint venture partners.

ESTABLISH OWNERSHIP, VALIDITY AND SUFFICIENCY

Establishing ownership

Trace the IPRs which the target company thinks it owns back to the original development. Inspect all assignments and any other transfer documents from the original registration or grant of the rights through to the target company:

- Has the target company respected employee rights to invention?

- Have contractors' rights been correctly assigned to the target company? Rights in inventions and copyrights belong to their creator.

- Have other individuals' rights been properly dealt with? Don't forget the founders – have they assigned rights to the company?

Are there any other issues with ownership of intellectual property? For example, shareware often comes with a host of restrictions on its use in other products.

Intellectual property may have to be assigned or licensed as part of the deal if the target company is being sold out of a group. It is not uncommon for several companies to use rights which are owned and registered by only one of them.

Third party agreements. Title may also be affected by the terms on which technology has been licensed from third parties. In particular, the future of the target may be seriously undermined by:

- Conditions limiting the right of the target to modify or adapt any licensed technology.

- Change of control clauses in the licensing agreement.

Has the seller encumbered the rights?

Establishing validity

Are all patents owned by the target active? Are other rights registered?

Do third parties have any rights in any jurisdictions in which you want to extend the target's operations?

Can rights be registered in other jurisdictions?

For both existing patents and patents pending, is the idea genuinely novel or is it likely to be challenged in the future?

Have all maintenance fees been paid? If not, patents the target thought it had may well have lapsed.

Has the target received infringement claims from third parties?

Where the target is a licensee of intellectual property, are all the important licences to which the target is party adequate?

Establishing sufficiency

Use technical and commercial investigations to assess:

- The extent of the competitive advantage brought by IPRs.

- Whether this is likely to last:
  - Can the protection be 'got round', say, by reverse engineering.
  - What alternatives do customers have to the target's IPRs?
  - Are there competitors with products/processes which achieve the same result but in a different way? That is without infringing the target's protected rights?
  - How long it would take for a reasonably competent competitor to replicate it and then decide what to do as far as the deal is concerned.

LICENCES

List by type of licence:

- Non-exclusive. Non-exclusivity gives the licensee no protection from competition.

- Sole. A sole licence protects the licensee from other licensees but not from competition from the licensor itself.

- Exclusive. If competition laws allow a licensee to get away with it, an exclusive licence protects the licensee from all competition.

Assess whether licences are adequate bearing in mind what will be needed in the future.

Do the licences cover the right territories?

Are rights sufficiently protected in those territories?

Do the licences cover everything needed? It is not unusual for rights to be confined to a particular field of application.

Are there unacceptable restrictions?

How are royalty payments calculated?

Are they reasonable?

Can royalty calculations be manipulated?

Do the royalty payments give/allow the target to make a reasonable return?

What are the obligations to maintain the rights, for example is there a responsibility for paying renewal fees?

Are there obligations to disclose improvements and rights to use those improvements.

Are there restrictions on developing alternative technology?

What is the duration of the licences? Do they last long enough?

Are there any conditions which would end the licence or its exclusivity (minimum sales targets for example)?

Is the licensor infringing third party rights? (It will be impossible to verify that the licensor owns all the rights therefore an indemnity to cover third party infringement claims may be required.)

Are there change of control clauses?

If so, are there clauses which restrict assignment?

Can consent to assign be obtained before completion?

Are there likely to be any competition issues? (An exclusive licence can have the effect of carving up a territory which competition authorities prohibit.)

What are the termination conditions?

Are there any outstanding breaches of licence conditions?

TRADEMARKS AND COPYRIGHTS

Has there been any non-use of trademarks? For what period of time?

Has there been any prior assignment of trademarks?

TRADE SECRETS

To the extent possible, identify all trade secrets and know-how used in or associated with the acquired business. Particularly, identify confidential information that the target has acquired from third parties.

Identify the target's procedures for protecting confidential information.

Identify the target's procedures for releasing information, for example in marketing materials or technical symposia.

Antitrust Due Diligence

OBJECTIVES

Prepare merger control filing requirements and assess the likelihood of clearance.

Assess the antitrust risks posed by the target's activities, that is the risk of buying into an infringement.

Review the enforceability of the target's contracts from the standpoint of antitrust law.

16.1 Merger Control Filing Requirements

Is the transaction subject to merger control? In which jurisdictions? *137*

What information is required for antitrust filings?

For a transaction directly involving one or more countries in the European Union, the legal advisers will need, as a minimum, the following information (the list is not-exhaustive):

- The turnover (net sales revenues) of each group in the following geographical areas:
    - worldwide;
    - EU;
    - EEA;
    - national in each EU and EEA country;
    - national in each other European country where either of the groups involved has operations.

- Information to determine the 'relevant' markets, and for each relevant market:
    - The parties' estimates of market size.
    - The revenues of each of the parties' groups in each market.
    - Estimates of competitors' market shares in each market.

- Overlapping or vertically-related products/services of the parties.

- Identification of demand and supply substitutes for each such product/service.

16.2 Antitrust Risks Posed by the Target's Activities

Is there any evidence of activities which could directly or indirectly fix purchase or selling prices or any trading conditions through:

- Abuse of dominant position?

- Market sharing or price fixing arrangements with competitors?

- Resale price maintenance? A vertical arrangement under which a supplier requires a purchaser to resell goods at a certain price.

- Limits or control over production, marketing, technical development or investment.

- Shared sources of supply.

- Sensitive information which is shared with competitors?

- Dissimilar conditions in equivalent transactions?

- Contracts which are subject to acceptance by the other parties of supplementary obligations which, by their nature or according to commercial usage, have no connection with the subject of such contracts. This would include, for example, making it a condition that a customer for product A buys product B before it is supplied with product A.

- Has the target terminated, or threatened to terminate, dealers because of their pricing or parallel importing or exporting practices?

In EU transactions, are there:

- Absolute territorial protection of exclusive distributors?

- Export restrictions within the EU?

Both of these are designed to prevent national economic frontiers from being recreated by business agreements.

There will be no written records of anti-competitive behaviour. It is, therefore, vital for the due diligence team to get out and talk to those people in the target who have the contact with the competition. Any commercial relationships between the target and its competitors (for example, in supply, licensing or joint venture agreements) should also be examined, along with any side deals that go with them.

ENFORCEABILITY OF CONTRACTS

Where there is trade across European borders, Article 81 of the EC Treaty says that clauses of an agreement which restrict competition cannot be enforced. Buyers should, therefore, ensure that the target has not negotiated anything which violates Article 81. Article 81 does, however, allow certain 'block' exemptions where agreements improve the production or distribution of goods or promote technical or economic progress and at the same time give a fair share of the benefits to consumers.

Block exemptions relate to:

- Exclusive distribution.

- Selective distribution, where the supplier appoints dealers on the basis of technical qualifications, the suitability of trading premises and stipulates that such dealers must not to sell to unqualified dealers.

- Exclusive purchasing.

- Patent licensing.

- Motor vehicle distribution and servicing.

- Research and development.

- Specialization.

- Know-how licensing.

- Franchising.

- Subcontracting arrangements.

- Joint venture agreements involving:
    - R&D;
    - production.

Insurance and Risk Management Due Diligence

OBJECTIVE

The objective of insurance and risk management due diligence is to assess present, future and, most importantly, past exposures of the business and dimension the structure and cost of the existing insurance programme.

CHECKLIST 17

Insurance and Risk Management Due Diligence

PAST, PRESENT AND FUTURE EXPOSURES

Establish an accurate insurance history.

How does the target address the following:

- The identification of risk?

- The evaluation of risk?

- The reduction of risk?

- The prevention of loss?

- How losses are reviewed:
    - Centrally?
    - In the business units?

- The measures being taken to reduce losses:
    - Frequency?
    - Magnitude?

- Disaster planning? What is its current status?

- Health and safety programmes? Are any planned? What are their status?

THE STRUCTURE AND COST OF THE EXISTING INSURANCE PROGRAMME

What are the existing arrangements?

What is the level of self-insurance? Does this represent an acceptable balance between cost and risk?

What is the extent and nature of third party insurance? On what basis?

- Occurrence/claims arising – covers incidents which occur during the policy period.

- Claims made – covers claims made while the policy is still in force.

*For Product Safety Concerns and Information please contact
our EU representative GPSR@taylorandfrancis.com Taylor & Francis
Verlag GmbH, Kaufingerstraße 24, 80331 München, Germany*

T - #0110 - 230425 - C0 - 246/174/8 - PB - 9780566088629 - Gloss Lamination